Please Don't Say
ANYTHING!
Don't Start Any
TROUBLE!

I'm grateful that the writer of this book has taken the time to share her story. When I read the first draft, I was moved not just because I am a person who saw them immediately after the news of their loss, but read of other challenging and painful moments growing up in an abusive family relationship. One of the remarkable things that help all of us is when people have the courage to share their stories. I have had a front seat to this family's pain since their son passed. Their journey has brought them to the place of asking all the questions: Why God? Getting angry at God, sleepless nights, mental anguish and grabbing for anything that will help keep them afloat. There are no quick answers, there is no remedy that will remove all the pain and suffering for such a significant loss, but there're is hope and grace from a God who does want to walk with us through our pain. There are insights and special nuggets found in people who have walked through dark times.

—Pastor Fred Sindorf

Please Don't Say ANYTHING! Don't Start Any TROUBLE!

J. ROSE GIBSON

WESTBOW®
PRESS
A DIVISION OF THOMAS NELSON
& ZONDERVAN

WestBow Press books may be ordered through booksellers or by contacting:

WestBow Press
A Division of Thomas Nelson & Zondervan
1663 Liberty Drive
Bloomington, IN 47403
www.westbowpress.com
1 (866) 928-1240

Because of the dynamic nature of the Internet, any web addresses or links contained in this book may have changed since publication and may no longer be valid. The views expressed in this work are solely those of the author and do not necessarily reflect the views of the publisher, and the publisher hereby disclaims any responsibility for them.

ISBN: 978-1-4908-6513-3 (sc)
ISBN: 978-1-4908-6515-7 (hc)
ISBN: 978-1-4908-6514-0 (e)

Library of Congress Control Number: 2015900368

Printed in the United States of America.

WestBow Press rev. date: 01/22/2015

Contents

Acknowledgments

Thank you to all who have helped me accomplish the writing of this book. Thanks, Big Al, for all your support and love. Thanks to Pastor Fred and Wanda, Pastor Bill and Marney Scully, Blossom Brown, Van and Marie Catron and Dr. A. Zofakis. Thanks to Shirlene Baker and to her family for allowing her to give so much time to help others.

Thank you, Kimberly and Gina, for all your love. Thank you, Alan, Jules, Julie, Olivia, and Helena.

Gerrie and Linda, Timmy, Larry, Kenny, and Janet, my good friends, I thank you.

Auntie June, Auntie Virgie, and Auntie Trudy, thank you all. And thanks to the Dominican, Franciscan, and Felician nuns, especially Sister Consorcia, who introduced me to Jesus.

Thanks to Pat Rankin and Julie Libreri for artwork and Kim P.T. for back cover photo. Thanks to LeeAnn and George Huebner for emotional and technical support. Thanks to Lee Ann Maurides for prayers. Thanks to Karen Sanders of Sanders IT Consulting Inc. for technical support. Thanks to all the people at WestBow Press who were so patient with me.

Scripture quotations, unless otherwise noted, are from the *Life Application Study Bible, New Living Translation,* second edition, copyright 1996: Used by permission of Tyndale House Publishers, Inc., Wheaton, IL 60189, USA. All rights reserved.

The cover image, "The Shape of Intimate Illusion," is the copyright of Rafal Olbinski. Image is courtesy of Patinae, Inc. (www.patinae.com).

Special thanks to Rafal Olbinski: Dziękuję i Bóg zapłać.

Introduction

This book is based on a true story, although names and places have been changed. This book tells the story of my life, the story of my immeasurable loss. It is a story of being forgiven and forgiving. It is a story of learning to be nice to each other and treasure every moment for each day brings new hope. I write this to let the world know that even though darkness surrounds, there is hope.

Many of the songs I mention are songs I heard my grandma sing. "He" (written by Richard Mullan), "I Believe" (written by Ervin Drake), "You'll Never Walk Alone" (written by Richard Rodgers and Oscar Hammerstein) and "Cool Water" (written by Bob Nolan) sometimes you could hear them on the radio, or else some cowboy on television was singing these songs. The songs have stayed with me all these years. I always felt that they were like prayers.

"When We Dance" (written by Sting) was a song that has significant lines that seem to have been written just for me.

The cover of this book has very special meaning. It is a print that Charlie, my husband and I bought for Justin, our son and Sarah, his fiancée as a wedding gift. We saw it as a portrayal of Justin and Sarah, depicting that they were to marry and live happily ever after as they both made their way to heaven.

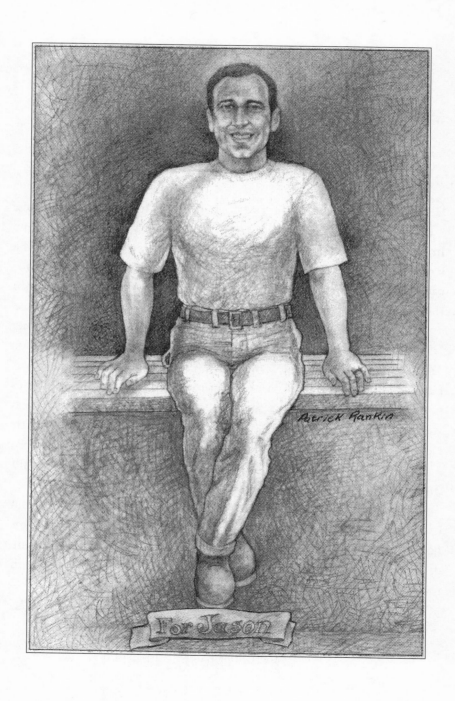

For Jason

Preface

The first thing I remember being told by my mother was "Don't say anything, don't start any trouble." This was family law and my brothers and sisters learned the same thing. We constantly said it to each other and even to my mother. Everything that we experienced while growing up was to be zip locked behind our lips. The horrible things we all experienced bent and crippled us and in my case may have caused me to lose my beautiful, innocent son. But I never said anything, never wanted to cause any trouble. This was my prison, a prison with no bars and no locks. With God's help, I found the way to tear down the bars, open the locks. I am now free; but for my son, it is too late. He is gone to live with a better parent, Jesus. I believe that God wants me to write this story because it may help at least one person find the way out of their prison and the way home to Him. I do believe that for "everyone who goes astray, someone will come to show the way" ("I Believe").

I wish that I still had my son here, but I guess that God wanted him back. I must accept this. As my dreams for the future are tossed and blown in a hurricane, I hold on to hope and strength in God. Someday, I will be reunited with my boy—and all my family—in heaven, where we'll live with Jesus for all eternity.

The Call, 2013

I remember the call. It was a Saturday morning in September. She was hysterical. "Help, he's gone! Justin's gone!"

"What do you mean, gone? Where would he go?" I asked.

"No, no! Something's wrong. He's gone, he's …" Sarah's voice trailed off. I couldn't hear the rest of what she was saying. I didn't want to. *Oh God, no!* It was impossible. My son, Justin, and I had just talked a few hours ago. I told Sarah that, no, he wasn't gone. I told her to hang up and call 9-1-1. Then, I hung up on her.

She called back right away. "I did. I called 9-1-1. I did. They're here now. He's gone. Oh God, he's gone."

But she didn't say *gone*. She used the *d* word, a word that I cannot say, let alone write.

Her tears and cries faded in my mind. I refused to believe what she had said. I heard screaming and realized that it was me. Why had I answered the phone? If I would have let it ring, then this would not have been true.

Sarah kept calling. *Stop calling me with this lie!* I kept hanging up until my husband, Charlie, took the phone.

It can't be. My son's gone? In a moment, tragically, suddenly, he was gone. My poor daughter-in-law was alone, frantic, grief-stricken.

Wait. He was only forty-two. It's a mistake. Older people are the first to go. It's me they want, not him! I can't breathe. I want to scream. Life is being wrung out of my heart. I can't believe it. My mind is a tornado. What can I do?

Above all, I had to let my son know that I loved him. I needed to tell him. I called out to him over and over, saying, "Go to Jesus. Fly to Jesus. Go to Jesus."

He could hear me. I knew it. They'd revive him by the time my husband and I got there. *Oh, please, revive him.*

We left on a plane immediately for California to see if this was real. For hours, Charlie and I cried, praying that this was all a big mix-up.

I looked out the plane window. *Oh, baby, are you there? Can you see me from the clouds? Do you hear me? Be with Jesus. Oh, let Him take care of you.* I was convinced that what Sarah had said wasn't true; it couldn't be. My boy was not gone. But when my husband and I made it to California, we found out that it wasn't a mistake.

I fell to the floor, but that didn't help.

We knew that Justin was with Jesus.

His wife was crippled with grief. We held her close, but our grief was so profound that only the arms of Jesus could offer us comfort.

"Jesus, where are you?" I screamed. "Why did you do this to us?"

My heart stopped. The blood ran out of my veins. My bones got cold. The pain was too much. *Let the whole world stop! Move back the clock! Hold back the earth, like Superman does! I want him back! I want my baby back! Why God, why? I'm not asking, "Why me?" I'm asking, "Why not me, God, why not me? Why him? Why did you take him? You can make a trade right now! No one will notice! You're God, so you can do it! You did it for Lazarus. My boy is worthy, too!"*

But God was silent. Not a word, not a rumble of thunder; just silence.

Justin had been married for only six months. He'd been way too young to leave us so soon. He had the perfect wife. She was the only one with whom he ever fell in love. Charlie and I loved her so. How could we take this pain from her? How could we take the pain from us?

We had so much to look forward to: the embryos growing into babies, a family. Sarah and Justin had had plans to buy a little house in Wisconsin so they could visit us more often. They'd prayed for those things. But God had not given them what they had prayed for. *They did nothing wrong! They were innocent children!*

Some people live long lives and never pray. People who have been married for years don't pray. Some people throw their babies into garbage cans! But it seems that these people still have all they want. *My son was a good man. His wife is a good person. Why, why, why?*

I knew that people died every day. Why was I making a big deal about one person? He was nobody. What had been so special about him that would make the world want to stop and turn backward in time so he could come back? Maybe God didn't care.

I thought that if I screamed loud enough or cried hard enough, God would send Justin back. I closed my eyes and screamed my son's name so loudly that I lost my voice. I scratched my face so deeply that it bled. I banged my head against the wall. I punched my chest, hoping that Jesus would hear me or at least take me to see Justin.

But it didn't happen. Justin didn't come back. I opened my eyes to see emptiness. No Jesus, no Justin. No words from God. No one cared. People weren't gathering outside. No reporters were asking for interviews, and no fans stood by with teddy bears or flowers.

My son hadn't been famous. He hadn't been rich. He hadn't earned any medals for playing sports. He hadn't won any contests or played in a rock band. He hadn't been an *American Idol* finalist. To the world, he was no one important.

But I cared. To me, he'd been the world. To Sarah, he'd been the world. He'd been Sarah's husband and my son and that was everything.

Though Justin and Sarah lived in California and Charlie and I lived in Wisconsin, we talked almost every day. Justin's was the call I looked forward to. It usually came around the same time every day. I got into a habit of making myself available at that time.

We talked about movies and exchanged reviews. We talked about the movie he was going to make. We laughed about Lifetime Movies, critiqued new movies, and he told me how much fun it was to work as a body double one time for Keanu Reeves.

We talked about life and the hopes and dreams that he and his wife had. We talked about my future grandchildren. We talked about God. We talked about that special little church in Califirnia where it was said Marilyn Monroe married Joe DiMaggio. I told him that there was something special about that church. He promised to visit it one day.

Justin was the one I'd go to with all my computer questions. He talked me through all the connection instructions and told me which e-mails were legitimate and which weren't. He told me about computer viruses and how to avoid them.

Twenty years ago, he designed and built a website for Charlie's business, before we even thought we needed it. He updated it frequently. The website sits dormant now, as if it's in mourning. I can do nothing with it. My heart breaks when I see it.

My son sent me e-mails. He sent me birthday cards. They weren't generic cards but special one-of-a-kinds. He always wrote me little messages, too. I still have the cards, but they don't fill the emptiness I feel.

Charlie and I had planned a special wedding celebration for Justin and Sarah at Christmas. Justin, Sarah, and I were planning a surprise seventy-fifth birthday party for Charlie.

All the plans were gone now, leaving us here with nothing but a future of blackness ahead.

Justin, my innocent child, I thought you would always be here.

Justin used to talk to me about his fears and concerns. He wanted to please people, wanting them to like him. It really bothered him when people didn't like him. He had a little delicate soul that made him worry about things like that.

He was the one who was there when I was sad. He really cared. He always had some consolation to offer and would top it off with a funny joke. He made me laugh. We talked about everything from financial planning to what type of paint to use on the deck.

He was very creative; he wrote, and directed his own shows. And he and Sarah produced those shows from time to time in theaters. He wrote a screenplay that he was just about to put into production.

From the time he was a little kid, Justin liked to draw little comic strips, thinking that one day he would put them into print. I look at them now and realize the tremendous talent he had.

While doing all these things, he also started a business called Justin's Painting and Decorating. He had five-star reviews on Yelp and Angie's List. He was very meticulous about his work, which was high quality. His specialty was wallpaper installation, at which he was quite skilled. Many of Los Angeles's top designers used him exclusively to do their work. He was able to make a good living with his lifetime partner, Sarah, who helped him on his jobs from time to time. They were both creative and made time for doing shows and their regular day jobs. They had been with each other for thirteen years. Their love was the real thing.

But I knew there was a shadow following my son. He talked about being afraid of something, someone in his building, someone who was relentless in tormenting him. Though he tried to shrug it off, he couldn't. He lived his life day to day hoping and praying that this feeling would go away.

I told him not to be concerned, that there were bullies like that everywhere, that he should ignore it. But it was more than that. Justin's problem was a thing that looked to sue everyone for anything and everything. It was a sinister being looking for an easy kill. It was a filthy, greedy thing disguised as a person—his neighbor, in fact—who would do whatever it took to add another coin to its bloated belly.

One day, this person actually told Justin that it wouldn't be satisfied until it owned every unit in the building. The bully promised my son, "One way or another, I'll get what I want."

The thing—I suppose I should say "neighbor"—often threatened to sue not only my son and his wife but also several others in the building. Even though the neighbor wasn't an attorney, she told Justin, "This is what I do for a living, sue people; I have connections and I always win." Justin was so afraid that she would find something to sue him for, some way to get the little money that he and Sarah had saved. It bothered him all the time. Justin and Sarah worked very hard to save for a child. Justin was constantly worried about the neighbor's threats.

I told him that one day that monster would tire and leave him alone. But she didn't. She gathered more energy as time went on, feeding on his misery.

I had no idea how insidious it was.

The woman enjoyed causing Justin so much grief at every turn, every day, locking doors, tossing wet laundry on the floor, tripping elevators, sending mysterious e-mails and slipping notes under the door, calling police with false accusations, and threatening lawsuit after lawsuit. Like a vampire, she even came to Justin's door one time, begging entrance to his home and asking to use his phone, a very strange thing nowadays, as most people have cell phones.

One time he saw her on his fire escape trying to open a window.

Thank God that he refused her entry. But in the end, I guess it didn't matter.

The neighbor saw Justin's innocence and watched him with the stealth of a salivating hyena, silently, relentlessly, on the hunt.

Justin tried to build up a shell around him for protection. He tried to appear tough and not show how much the woman bothered him. But this thing didn't let up. She tormented him daily. He ultimately knew that there was no escaping.

When the problem wouldn't go away, Justin sought legal help. But the system failed him. When he finally recognized that he was powerless against this evil, he tried to run away as far and as fast as possible. He was only one week from getting away. But he could not outrun this animal stalking its prey, smelling his few dollars as if blood were in the air.

This thing tormented my son, roaring out lies, pouncing on him, filling her mouth with blood, and rolling in a frenzied orgasm on a bed of money with her demon cohorts.

The doctors failed Justin. The hospital failed him. But most important, I failed him.

I asked myself if the one who feasted on his pain would receive the full measure of God's punishment. When will the justice come?

My eyes burn with tears and rage while the minions of Satan live and breathe. I can't believe that God let this abomination live and rob my son of his life and his small savings, leaving a grieving widow with nothing.

But it was my fault! I had seen the situation but had downplayed it, telling Justin not to worry, that everything would be alright.

I feel that I failed to guard my son from that jackal. I should have seen it coming. I should have destroyed her!

But demons are sly. They go for the innocent, the lame, those with afflictions. These demons dress in soft blue flowered clothing and rich perfume to disguise their stench. They stay far away from anyone who could threaten them.

Eternity is a long time. I pray that justice will come soon for those who made Justin's last days so miserable.

Questions

My heart breaks when I can't think of the plans that Justin and I had made for the future! This is not the right order of life, oh no. Moms and dads should go first, not kids.

I'd give the world for the opportunity to change places with my son. Why can't it be? My broken heart is full of guilt and torture. Could I have spared him the anguish? Could I have helped him be more resilient?

I prayed for him and all my children, as most any mother would do. But I never prayed for his wealth or success. I always prayed for Justin and Sarah's eternal salvation. That was most important to me. I wanted us to all meet up in heaven and be happy. I didn't want any of them to go so soon. Maybe I should have prayed for more protection for them in this life.

All I can do is look back and wonder if I could have changed anything in Justin's life, made any part of it better, spent more time with him, been a better mom, helped him more than I did.

I'm lost.

Had he been taken from me as a punishment for my sins? Was this God's way of getting even with me for all the bad things I'd done? Are my sins visited upon my boy? "That's not fair," I cry out to the Lord. "Punish me, not my son! It's not too late. You're God! You perform miracles all the time! You can still make this happen! Prove to me you are really God!"

But I hear Him say, "You don't tempt the Lord."

Then, He is silent.

I try another approach, something a little more meek: *God, forgive me for everything bad I've done!* But that doesn't change anything. I hear nothing, total silence—not a word, not a sign.

How does God work these things out? How am I supposed to understand Him? I thought that He loved my son. I thought that He loved my son's wife. I thought that He loved me. But now I'm not so sure. All I get from Him is, "You don't tempt the Lord."

And that's it. He's gone. God has left the building. *Ha!*

This grief, this torment, minute after minute, day after day, never leaves. Is this what hell is?

All the bad things I've done come back to me. I feel that heaven and hell are laughing at my pain after having taken everything from me. I feel alone, bad, and unworthy of any happiness or hope.

When I look back, when I remember what people said about me, I realize that I've been bad since I was a little girl, so maybe this tragedy is a just punishment. I thought I was good. For a while, I thought I was great. But I guess it was true what mom and dad said—I was bad, as bad as you can get.

So now, God gets revenge. It's my punishment. He took my son in exchange for my sins. I know it's true that I may have forgotten about God for a while, but I thought I came back to Him of my own volition.

He helped me escape the Devil long ago, or so I thought. I thought I left the Devil in hell, still counting as the singing stopped and the cage door flew open, but maybe not soon enough.

I thought God had forgiven me. Have I asked for too much? I just want my whole family together. I thought we'd all grow old together. But He took that. Is he a father like my own father on earth? My faith is shaken.

Didn't I have enough faith in God? Or did I have too much and He decided to test me? But why would God feel that I needed a test? I know many people who have strong faith, and they haven't suffered any such loss.

And I know many people who don't believe in God at all and are living long lives with no such loss. They seem pretty happy. And now I know that there are people who have been demonized and are allowed to continue their existence with no regrets.

So, are all the people who experience grief the ones God doesn't like? Does He enjoy hurting them?

Suddenly, I'm aware that such grief exists. It seems to be all around me, suppressing the air I breathe. I see the news every day. I see too much sadness, too many innocent people experiencing so much grief. I see families torn apart by random bullets and so many children just thrown away like garbage. I see other moms cry and I understand.

Why do I feel grief so strongly now? I see injustice. I see all of these grieving people now. My shell has been stripped away. The veil is lifted and my eyes flash open. I cry for others' sorrow even though I don't know them. They don't deserve it, either. Or do they?

But then I think *what do we human beings deserve?*

I know, I know. We deserve nothing from God. He doesn't owe us even the air we breathe. He gives it because He loves us. Yeah.

Does this mean that when He takes your breath away, He doesn't love you? How can I make myself realize God's love after this? Did He spend all His love on all those other people from the bible? Is there none left?

I answer my questions with more questions. Whereas before, I thought I had all the answers, I now need to find if they're true. No one can help me. I'm alone. I cannot breathe, I cannot see, I cannot hear. I need my heart to beat again.

Everything in my heart and soul tells me that my son was good and is now in heaven. That I believe.

First John 4:14–15 reads, "And we are confident that He hears us whenever we ask for anything that pleases Him. And since we know He hears us when we make our requests, we also know that He will give us what we ask for."

I know that it is God's will that every soul be in heaven. I always prayed that my family would be in heaven but not now, not like this. Did I pray him to be "gone"? My prayers are answered for my son. I think that that is the only part I believe anymore.

I don't think I'll make it. Not now, not the way I feel.

Me? I'm bad, unworthy, guilty. I'm convinced that it's my fault that my son is gone. I may never get to heaven, given the way I feel now—bitter, sad, depressed, tormented, and angry with God. But if I want to see my son again in heaven, even if there's just a small chance, then I need to resolve this problem between God and me.

I'm doomed without the right answers. I'm supposed to accept that I'll never understand why God does what He does. Is it just that easy?

I try to compare my mind to that of my little pet dog, Iris. No matter how long she lives or how many tricks she learns, she will never understand humans. She just trusts and loves; she never questions where she gets her food, where we go all day, why the sun comes up. She just jumps into my lap and loves me, trusts me, loves me, and is loved back.

I know that's what I'm supposed to do, just jump into God's lap and love and trust Him. I could be like Abraham and tell Him, "Yeah it's okay, take my son, go ahead." But God stopped Abraham and didn't take Isaac. He did take Justin.

Why?

And what if God doesn't want me? What if I've already failed the test? It's not easy to get back to a place of innocence, a place of innocent, simple belief, especially with the Devil leaning on the wall, juggling his rings, laughing, and saying, "Should have stuck with me, kid."

I tell the Devil to go back to hell. He leaves for a while but then returns to torture me with guilt.

Do I exact revenge upon the woman who hurt my son? Is it up to me? Was it up to me to protect him from that evil? Am I worse than she is? How will that predator pay? Is it up to me to make her pay? If I do, then who will make me pay? Will God forget about this by the time that woman dies and faces Him? Will He just figure that in the scheme of things, what she did was no big deal and then let it go? Does all this pain sorrow mean nothing?

I can't let this continue. Why, why, why? Why do I feel that God has abandoned me? I'm going to have to go back to that place where I felt He loved me, that child like place of accepting that there are things I'll never know, that place where I don't try to out think God.

But can I? I wasn't a good child. Alright, I know that. I wasn't a good young adult, either. So, it follows that I was not a good parent, not a good anything.

I'm worthless. How much happiness did I rob from my son's life? Why did I allow others to rob him? I'm done living, done with it all. Why can't I just die?

Before I decide to end it all, it's time to take a good look at my life and take the punishment I deserve, take it all with me throughout eternity, wear those chains, feel that fire. I must own up to it. Just in case I don't like the answers, I take a sharp knife—just in case it's too horrible to face, just in case, just in case.

Was God ever with me throughout my lifetime? If He was, then what made Him leave me? Who am I now? I'm not me anymore. What am I supposed to do with my shattered life? How do I retrieve a faith that now needs to be made strong as welded iron, not just folded paper taped and glued together? Was my faith ever there?

I think I need to see where I've been, slop through the muck and mire of the past and try to find what I need. I need to see if there are any bouquets of good memories left to pick, and then I need to bring those flowers back and harvest a lesson from them. If there are no flowers, there is no me. I must look back to see if I can find answers, because, so far, all I do is ask more questions.

Why did God abandon me in this, the most difficult time of my life? Why? Why? All my life other people always told me what to do, and I listened. Now, there's no one to tell me what to do. I'm on my own. And the same answer keeps coming up: It's my fault.

If I let this guilt consume me, then I'll be lost forever and never see my son again. I know that unless I have God, the real God, in my heart, in my life, my life is not worth living.

"But that's why we brought the knife. I'll show you that your life is worthless and you belong to me," the Devil whispers in my ear. I can hear *him* alright.

My heart is hollow. The Devil awaits me. "Who is that God? Where is He now?" he asks.

But I hear something else …something far, far away. I know the words and remember the tune from long ago. I can barely hear it from an old radio. Gene Autry or some other cowboy is singing, "Don't listen to him, Dan. He's the Devil, not a man, and he spreads the burning sand with water, cool, clear water. Old Dan and I with throats burned dry and souls that cry for water …" The song fades in the distance.

God, my soul cries for water!

God where is He? I'm not sure, not right now.

I wonder if it's like my dad said: "When you're gone, you're gone. That's all there is."

Or maybe it's like my mother said: "You never really die. You just turn into something else: a bird or an animal, even a bug."

But that can't be all there is. And I don't want to be a bug!

Others say that it's karma, that you get back what you give. But had I been so bad that this torture was what I got in return?

I knew the truth at one time. At one time, I really did. But it's so confusing now. I need to find peace. I want to, I really want to renew that commitment in my soul, but just in case, just in case, I reach into my pocket and feel the wooden handle. It's there, just in case.

But first I need to find out where I went wrong and why. I'm not sure it's a road I want to travel. I'm not sure it's a picture I want to see.

So, who can help me?

The Little Girl

There was a little girl, I remember. Maybe it was that little girl's fault. Maybe she was the bad one and I'm taking the punishment for her. Am I supposed to find her?

I remember things from long ago about her: that scared little girl hiding under the covers, clutching her statue of Jesus, and praying, "Please, don't say anything; please, don't start any trouble." Scared, so scared …

Why do I remember her? Who was she, and why do I feel that I need her so badly? Maybe if I can find her, if she's still there, then she'll tell me why she was so frightened. Had I scared her?

I left her long ago. She was nothing to me, a worthless nothing. That's why I left her. I don't even know if I'm sorry for leaving her—or if it even matters.

But something tells me I should be sorry. Something tells me I need her forgiveness. Would she forgive me for leaving her alone so many years ago? Would she talk to me? I have so many questions that only she could answer. I never let her talk to anyone else. I kept her a prisoner, locked up, told her not to say anything, not to cause any trouble. I was the only one she ever knew.

It seems that I took her somewhere never to be found, pushed her down and then locked the door. Maybe I killed her. She was a bad girl and caused lots of trouble so she probably deserved to be killed. I didn't like her, anyway. No one liked her. If I find it is her fault that Justin is gone, then what will I do?

Too many years have gone by. There may be nothing left of that little girl. I'm lost and scared. But if she's gone forever, if that's true, then somehow I know that I'll be gone forever, too. And I don't care! Let me just fade away from all this.

I turn around to look at a faded black landscape. *Is this what my past looks like?* It's dark. There's no clear path. I see shadows moving. Long, pointed teeth shine in the darkness. Monsters lurk, waiting to pounce. They would hurt me. They would hurt others, too.

But I know that the hurt ahead of me will be much greater if I go on alone and leave that little girl in the shadows, if she is even still there. I'll make her talk! I'll force the answers from her. If I discover that God is making me pay for her sins, I'll make her face the monsters and pay.

I need to find out. I need to know what she'd done, whatever the consequences. So, I make my way back into that shadowy swamp laced with webs alive with millions of spiders. I see the quicksand, the muck, and the lies. Back through the rotted wood, I find rusted cars, overgrown vines, screams, broken skeletons, and slithering snakes. Gingerly stepping over crushed rats, I return to dig out that scared little girl who is biting her fingernails and hiding under a rotting tree.

That's it! That's where I left her! If only I can find that old tree.

But with no food, no water, she couldn't after all this time … I freeze with fear. Something foreboding is in the air. The way into the swamp is overgrown, sinister, and ominous. The air is so heavy I can hardly breathe. Monsters, I can hear them, smell them. I don't want to see them again, but it's too late now.

I didn't want to see the—

Way off in the distance, I heard a little girl crying. *It can't be her after all these years.* She sounded like she was hurt.

"Water," she cried.

I ran to the sound. At the edge of the darkness, I hesitated, wondering if I would find the answers I wanted or find out something worse, something I didn't want to know. I realized that once I started in, there may be no way out.

I shrugged it off. It didn't really matter. I had nothing to lose. No one could hurt me any more than God had done by taking my son, my baby. Death would be a consolation for me. I reached into my pocket. I didn't care what awaited me.

I started in. After a few steps, I turned and saw that vines had closed off my escape route. There was no turning back. I was near her. We were in the swamp with souls that cried *for water ... cool, clear water.*

I called out, running, tripping, pushing off the cobwebs, shaking off the many spiders that fell out of the webs and were crawling on me. I didn't care. I followed her voice, so dim, so desperate.

I slid into a muddy hole. *Is this quicksand?* Under the old fallen tree, I saw her. The monsters had left so many bites that I hardly recognized her shape. Was this the bad girl I was looking for? What had she done to cause God to be angry and take my son? She looked like a monster herself. Her face was filthy, her body skinny and pale. Bones stuck out from her back. Her eyes were swollen closed. Her fingers and toes were bleeding. *No, this can't be the bad girl I'm looking for. What am I doing? I won't find any answers here.* I wanted to run.

It was too late. She knew I was there. Her clawlike fingers grabbed my hand. I heard a low, rustling sound coming from her, like dried leaves blowing in the wind. "Help me! Monsters ..." She held up her arm, which looked like something had just taken a bite out of it. Black blood oozed from the wound. I thought I saw something move, maggots. I quickly looked away. I didn't think she could stay there longer. *The monsters will soon gobble her up.*

Was I dreaming? I tried to awake but couldn't. Then I knew it was no dream. *It's real or sure seems to be. Am I here? Is this my past? Or is this my future?*

Before I could reason that out, I heard a sound, slight at first, then louder. It was surreal, so odd in that place. I could hear music, a tinny-sounding radio. It couldn't be, but it was true. I could hear Roy Rogers, or was it Gene Autry, singing. *Where was the radio? How did it get electricity?* "Old Dan and I with throats burned dry and souls that cry for water, cool, clear water." I could hear the scratches on the old 78 record. It was real.

She heard it, too. Her head turned toward the sound. She seemed to recognize the song. Her eyes looked up from their little slits and stared at me. It seemed that she recognized me, too.

"I was waiting for you," she whispered. Her voice was soft, gravelly, like rustling leaves in the wind. I could barely hear her.

"Me? Waiting for me? How? Why?" I moved closer. "Who are you? What's your name?"

"Will you help me? Will you help me get out of here?"

"I'll try, I'll try. But who are you? Why am I here?" At that point, I wasn't sure of anything. The girl didn't answer. She started shaking. She looked cold and too pathetic to be the bad girl I'd been looking for. I took off my sweater and wrapped it around her. We sat there for a while on the damp ground.

"It's okay. Don't be scared. Talk to me," I said. "Tell me how you got here." I had to bend my head down to hear her small voice.

"I can't. They'll hurt me if I tell," she said.

"Who, who will hurt you?"

"Monsters ... all monsters, they'll get me. You, you'll hurt me."

"Talk to me. Where are they? I won't let them hurt you. And I'm not here to hurt you. I came to find someone ..."

"I can't say anything. I don't want to cause any trouble," she whispered.

"No! You have to talk to me," I said. "You can talk. You won't cause any trouble. Tell me whatever you can. Are you the one I'm looking for? Who are you? Do you know me?"

"I ... I don't know you," she said. I wanted to leave and began to pull away from her. "Please, I'm scared. I've been alone here so long, so long. Please, stay, just a little. Please, don't hurt me." She whispered these things as she closed her eyes.

How could this broken little girl have helped me? It looked like she was the one who needed help. I decided I should stay a little while but that I wouldn't take too much time with her. After a bit, I'd be on my way. I thought maybe that if I did stay, she'd help me continue my search for the bad girl so I held her close for a long time before I fell asleep.

I awoke to a cool rain. I was disoriented. I was in a place I didn't belong, and I felt darkness all around, closing in on me. *I'm wasting time I really need to get out of here.*

The little girl was awake, too, looking at me with pleading eyes. I saw water puddled in some big leaves. I carefully reached for the leaves and offered her the water. She drank and gestured for more. I gave her more. "How long was I asleep? Where am I? What day is it? What kind of plane is that in the sky? For God's sake, I don't even know what year it is. I feel dizzy, in a fog. I don't belong here. I can't stay," I said.

I reached up to pull myself out of the hole. The little girl pushed my hands down into my lap and shook her head no. After a few minutes, she began to talk softly.

Charleston Street, 1953

"It was this morning you got here, I think, maybe Tuesday. I'm not sure, but I know it's 1953. I heard it on the radio."

"It can't be. It's impossible," I said. "Time doesn't go backward. If it did, then I ... I'd have another chance. I would ... he could ..."

The little girl looked at me sadly and shook her head. She turned her head and focused on a point in the distance. Her eyes were glazed, almost hypnotic, as she continued. "I was in my bedroom, waking up to sun streaming in from the kitchen window and the sound of Roy Rogers singing 'Cool Water' coming from the radio in my mom and dad's bedroom. Can't you see it? I know you hear it. Be still. Look."

I began to see. Out of the fog, forms began to take shape. Though the little girl was right next to me, I could see her clearly emerging from the fog in front of me. It was as if I were watching a television show and she was the narrator.

"My big sisters have already left for school. Next year, I'll be able to go to school. I had to wait till I was six to go to first grade. Kindergarten was for rich people. I had to stay home until I was six and could go to first grade. I was going to play dollhouse or tea party that day. Maybe Mommy would have time to play with me. That would be a lot more fun than playing alone.

"I needed to go to the bathroom, but Mommy said to stay in bed and be quiet. She warned me to wait until Daddy left for work. 'Listen, Lady Jane, you stay in bed and be quiet. Don't look to start trouble. You're always looking to start trouble!' Mommy told me.

"Daddy scared me. He was so big and so loud. I didn't want to get in his way because I'd be blamed for starting a fight. But I didn't think I could wait much longer. It really hurt. I had to go so bad. But I knew it would hurt more if I got to the bathroom and he decided to get up. So, I stayed in bed.

"Then I couldn't wait any longer! I thought I could be quick. I had to disobey. I got up and ran to the bathroom. I heard his footsteps heading to the bathroom. He kicked the door open. 'What's she doing in there? I gotta get to work. I can't wait around for these kids. I told you I don't want to see any of these kids around before I go to work. Get her out of here!' he yelled.

"I was in trouble! I'd done a bad thing. I jumped off the toilet. I wasn't finished, and it hurt to hold in the rest, but I tugged my pajama pants up and ran to bed.

"I started crying because my pajama bottoms were wet and I was scared. I knew I was in trouble. Mommy stuck her head into the room and told me to be quiet. She said that I'd been bad and caused a lot of trouble, that I should have listened to her and stayed in bed. I couldn't stop crying. She told me that if I shut up, she'd play dollhouse with me later after Daddy left. So I stuck my face in the pillow and cried very quietly.

"After what seemed like a long, long time, Daddy left for work. Then, Mommy let me get out of bed. She scolded me for the wet pajamas, but I didn't say anything to explain it. They dried out after a while. I'd already caused enough trouble.

"But Mommy did as she promised and played dollhouse with me. After that, she gave me some toothpicks and paste to play with while she made supper. I made a really nice house and boat, but I used up most of the toothpicks, so Mommy said I was done.

"Later that day, I heard Daddy's footsteps coming up the back porch. Mommy told me, 'Don't say anything! Go back to the bedroom and stay there under the covers just in case Daddy's still mad at you.'

"I didn't say anything, but then, when Daddy saw my toothpick house, he realized most of his toothpicks were gone. He was going to give me a beating for using all his toothpicks. I pretended to be asleep, so he left me alone. *You're a bad girl*, I told myself. But I didn't say anything and didn't cause any trouble, at least not that night."

The little girl hesitated, flinched, and stopped talking. She looked up at me.

"Please, tell me more. It's okay. I want to know all about you," I said, holding her closer.

Slowly, like the start of a soft rain, she continued. "We lived on the second floor over my grandma's house. She was my dad's mother. She let us live up there for free. My mom and dad got married in '42 or '43, whatever that means. At least, that's what I heard them say. I was third oldest of five kids when we lived there.

"Most of what I remember is that Mommy and Daddy had lots of fights that lasted till the middle of the night, sometimes till it got light out. Daddy liked to smoke and drink beer, and he'd usually drink a real lot. He said he had to drink a lot because he worked so hard. It was the only way he could relax, he said.

"I don't think Mommy ever relaxed, because she didn't drink or smoke. But I suspected that once in a while she hid in the bathroom to smoke, 'cause I could smell cigarette smoke … only one time though.

"Did I say something bad?" she asked. "I mean, I never saw anything, and I don't know for sure. I didn't mean anything bad about my mommy."

She started to cry.

"No, you didn't say anything wrong. It's fine," I said.

The little girl looked at me as if to ask if I wanted to hear more. I nodded yes, and then it was like a cloudburst. The little girl spoke fast. It was as though she had to tell me quickly before anyone else, maybe the monsters, heard and tried to stop her.

"Is it okay for me to tell you all this stuff? You won't tell on me, will you? You won't tell anyone, will you? Because if they hear…."

She didn't wait for my answer. I think she knew it. I couldn't make that promise. But it seemed that she didn't want to hear me say it.

"When Daddy had too much to drink, he kept everyone awake all night, sitting by his desk and really yelling about his money and how he never had enough of it. He would start out talking to himself until the talking got louder and louder. Sometimes, Grandma would bang on the ceiling downstairs for him to be quiet.

"He complained how food cost too much, schoolbooks were too expensive, electric bills were too much. Mommy spent too much on food. And he didn't have enough money for all of our stuff.

"'Five kids, five kids. I never wanted all these kids!' He would yell it over and over. 'Five mouths to feed. Five mouths to feed!' I felt bad. I knew I was one of the kids who made Mommy and Daddy fight.

"I wished I wasn't there, but I didn't know how to get away. I didn't know how to make it one less mouth to feed. Sometimes, I tried not to eat in order to save the food so that he could have more, but I got hungry too many times. I couldn't help it.

"We never knew when Daddy was going to start a fight. But whenever there were fights, they usually started in the evening after supper and lasted till early morning. Daddy would do a lot a swearing. Most of the things he said were really bad, and most were swearwords. We were told not to say anything if Daddy came in our bedroom yelling, which was often, to pretend we were sleeping. We told Mommy to please not start anything.

"Mostly, I'd cry quietly and bite my nails. First, it was fingers. Then, when they looked so bad that other people made fun of me, I'd bite my toenails so they couldn't see, but then I bit them so bad that it was painful to walk when I put my shoes on.

"It was hard for my two older sisters, Helen and Sadie, to get up and go to school after staying up almost the whole night listening to those loud fights. Mommy told them school wasn't important. They were just girls and would get married and stay home all day. They didn't have to learn anything. She said it was a waste for them to go to school. But they went whenever they could, anyway. They liked school. They had friends and looked forward to seeing them. They were happy going to school. I couldn't wait till it was my turn to go. I wanted to be happy like that.

"We had a small television my grandma gave us. I watched *Ding Dong School* with Miss Frances on television, but it seemed kind of babyish. I couldn't wait to get big enough to go to first grade.

"I watched some other kids' shows besides *Ding Dong School*, the baby show. *Romper Room* was really babyish. *Garfield Goose* was good, but I remember hearing my dad tell my mom, 'You know all these TV shows that talk so nice about boys and girls and kiddy games? The only reason they like kids is because they don't have any. If they had any kids of their own, they'd find out really fast how much they hated 'em.' It always made feel bad when he talked like that. So, I pretended I didn't hear. I knew he didn't want me, or any of us, around. I was scared to run away because I wouldn't have anywhere to sleep at night.

"Then, one day, it was my turn to go to real school. I remember heading out to first grade, not knowing what to expect. It was scary being there alone, but I kind of liked it. We did art projects and learned the ABCs, and I started learning how to read. But then I missed so much schooltime because of my parents' fights. I couldn't keep up with what I was supposed to be learning. Lots of kids laughed at me when the teacher asked me a question that I couldn't answer. But one of my favorite subjects was religion. I was good at answering questions about religion, even if I didn't study for it. I loved to hear stories about Jesus and the saints.

"We didn't pray at home except at bedtime. 'Now I lay me down to sleep.' We usually said that prayer. Sometimes, when the fights were so bad, I hoped that the part of that prayer, 'If I should die before I wake,' would come true.

"Mommy and Daddy didn't go to church, and they didn't make us go. My grandma downstairs talked about Jesus. She called him Bozia. I think that was the Polish word for 'Jesus.' And she taught me some songs. Want to hear some?"

I nodded.

"I remember only parts of them, so here goes. 'He lights every star that makes our darkness shine. He keeps watch all through the long and lonely night.' I don't know all the other words, but it ends with, 'He'll always say: "I forgive."'

"That's one. Another part I remember from one of the other songs: 'When you walk through the storm, hold your head up high, and don't be afraid of the dark.'

"There's more, but I can't sing it so good in front of anyone. I've kind of been singing that one for a long time now. There's lots more words, but those last ones kind of helped me in here all this time. This is another one I liked. 'I believe above the storm the smallest prayer can still be heard. I believe that someone in the great somewhere hears every word.' I believe, I believe, oh I do believe that!' I believed you'd come here."

"You have a very pretty voice, you know," I said.

"No, I know I don't, but that was nice to hear you say."

"No, really, I mean it."

"Nobody means anything they say. Stop it! Stop making fun of me."

The girl became quite angry. I wanted to explain. "I'm not making fun of you, really. I'm sorry you feel that way."

She paused for a bit before continuing.

"I thought about becoming a nun when I was in second grade. I loved to collect holy cards with pictures of Jesus or Mary or the saints. Mommy would always tell us to be nice to people and not to hurt anyone's feelings. She said that hurting someone would make Jesus cry. I didn't want to make Jesus sad. I didn't want to make anyone sad.

"Daddy was a deliveryman and a junk collector. He started his own business. Grandpa gave my dad some money to buy a truck which he used for moving whole houses of furniture for people and also for picking up junk. He always found a helper to help him with the big boxes and heavy items. I remember some of their names: Lefty, Google Eyes, Bee Bee, Tommy, Joey, and some guy who turned out to be a burglar and went to jail. The Chessman, I think they called him.

"My older sisters, Helen and Sadie, thought Joey was really cute. He was the only cute one. I thought he was cute, too. But I also remember that some of Daddy's helpers smelled a lot like old beer and smoke. One day, Lefty threw up on my feet in our car. It was really smelly, and my shoes always smelled kind of bad after that. In school, kids would say 'p.u.' and call me stinky-feet Jane. I was really happy when I outgrew those shoes!

"Daddy had advertising circulars that read, 'Free Free Free Estimates.' He'd drive around, and one of us kids would jump out of the car and drop off one or two at different stores and houses. Sometimes, if he had a delivery near the house, he would stop in at home for a quick lunch. My mother was always nervous because she never knew if or when he'd come home.

"If the house wasn't all cleaned up, he'd get mad. If she didn't have something he liked completely ready to eat, he'd yell at her. If she was listening to the phonograph, she quickly shut it off because he'd get mad that she was listening to records while he was out working.

"One time, I remember she made him some fried baloney. I asked her for some because I really liked fried baloney. But she said there wasn't enough. Mommy said that if there was any left over, then she'd make me a sandwich after my dad went back to work.

"Anyway, something about the sandwich—maybe too much mayonnaise or not enough or no butter—I don't remember. But he didn't like it. I remember him yelling at my mom and finally throwing the dish with the baloney sandwich at the wall. The dish broke and fell, but the baloney just stuck there on the wall.

"I was thinking the baloney was going to be wasted and I could have had some. But Mommy knew I wanted it, so, after he left the house, she washed it off and made me a sandwich. I was happy with the sandwich, but it wound up that I couldn't eat it all. I felt so sad about the fight that it made my stomach hurt.

"Mommy cried the rest of the day. She cried a lot of days. It made me sad. Mommy did a lot of things to try to make Daddy happy, but it seemed that he was always mad about everything.

"We had to have a phone so my mom could answer my daddy's calls and take messages about where he should pick up and deliver furniture or boxes. Mommy wasn't allowed to use it for her own calls.

"First, we had a phone with a party line, but that didn't work because the people who called him couldn't always get through. Do you know what a party line is?"

Although I knew, she seemed to want to tell me. So, I asked her what it was. She seemed proud that she knew the answer. She kind of smiled as she told me.

"It was a phone service you could get that was cheap, but you had to share the line with two or three other customers. So, when one customer was on the phone, you could hear them talking and were supposed to hang up and then make the call after the line was clear. None of the customers knew each other. I don't think they did. I heard Mommy say that, anyway.

"We were supposed to leave the phone alone, but I remember one time, my little brother Jack and I picked up the phone and heard some people talking. We were listening and laughing. Then the lady yelled, 'Hang up, you nosy—' She said a swearword at us! We laughed about that. No one else knew, so we didn't get in trouble.

"Me and my brother, we did lots of stuff like that! One day, we snuck in by my daddy's nightstand and found some books with pictures of naked girls. We laughed and put them back, getting out of there before anyone knew we'd found them."

The girl stopped abruptly. "You won't say anything, will you? I don't want to get in trouble. I don't want Jack to get in trouble."

"You won't get in trouble and he won't get in trouble." I said.

"Well, okay. Just forget what I said about that. I'll finish what I was telling you about the telephones. Promise not to tell?"

"Okay, I promise."

"One day, we got a pay phone installed. You put dimes and nickels in the top part and then you could make the call. But my dad didn't always have the change he needed to put in the phone. Also, he said that he didn't trust my mother with any money left around because she would steal it. So, we got a regular phone with a dial on it.

"Mommy was still not allowed to use it. She was only allowed to answer the calls. Daddy put a lock on the dial so she couldn't dial out. Sometimes, her mother or brother called, but she was not allowed to talk long because she had to keep the line open in case my dad called. Sometimes, Daddy would call from a phone booth just to check if the line was open.

"More than once, he came home yelling and screaming that he hadn't been able to get through because the line had been busy. He accused her of talking to her mother or brother. But most times, it was just because she was taking his messages. I knew because I was there. I was home from school a lot.

"Daddy had a checking account, but he wouldn't allow my mom to write checks. I wasn't sure what a checkbook was, but I knew it had to do with money. He always hid his checkbook or left it downstairs with my grandma. Sometimes, he would have extra money and would tell my grandma to hold it for him because he didn't trust my mommy.

"He told Mommy that when she went to work and could make enough money, she could use her money to support us and he could stay at home and laze around all day like she did. He said all the money was his because he was the only one who worked and slaved for it. Money, money, money! That's all he talked about, all the time.

"One time, I found a twenty-dollar bill on the sidewalk. Daddy said I had to give it to him because I was with him when I found it. I wanted to give some to Mommy and maybe keep some for me. I held the money in my hand and started to cry. Then Daddy said that he would write down three amounts on folded paper. He said one was for three dollars, one was for seventeen dollars, and one was for twenty dollars. He said the one I pull out would be the amount I get. He folded the papers and put them in a bowl so I couldn't see the numbers. Then, he told me to close my eyes and pick one out. I said a little prayer and picked out the one I hoped would say twenty dollars. But when I unfolded the paper, I saw it had a three on it. I was disappointed that I didn't win more money, but I told Mommy I would give it all to her. When I asked Daddy for the three dollars, he said he didn't have any change and would pay it to Mommy next week. Later, I looked in the garbage can and found the three folded papers. Each of them had a three marked on it. I showed them to Mommy and told her there was no seventeen or twenty written on any of them. She told me to be quiet and not to start any trouble. So, this is the first time I ever told anyone about that. I don't think that was a fair thing to do. But I didn't say anything because I didn't want to cause any trouble. I don't think Daddy ever gave the three dollars to Mommy. My mommy never had money. Daddy told us she was lazy, over and over and over. He told us she was a thief. He told anyone who would listen that she was a liar and a cheat. Sometimes, he'd go on the back porch and yell it out so the neighbors would hear.

"One time, one of the neighbors, Izzy, yelled back and told him to be quiet because he didn't want to hear my dad's problems. Daddy never liked him after that and warned him that he'd go over and punch him if he ever talked back to him again.

"Daddy gave Mommy 'pay' to get groceries only. She had no allowance for clothes or anything else. When we needed shoes or clothes, we'd have to ask him. After we did a lot of begging, he'd take us with Mommy to get what we needed.

"Sometimes, he wouldn't give her the 'pay.' That was when he was mad at her. Lots of times, we used pages from the phone book for toilet paper. The toilet paper was saved for my dad. He also had tooth powder to brush his teeth, but he said we didn't need it. He said we should use kitchen cleanser. He said he'd used it as a kid and it was good enough for him, so it should be good enough for us. I tried it, but it tasted kind of bad, so I didn't do that more than a couple of times.

"Sometimes, my dad's sisters would give my mother some of their makeup. Or she would be able to buy some for herself out of the grocery money if the makeup was cheap enough. I remember a little red case of Maybelline with a cake of black stuff in it. It came with a brush. Mommy used to wet it down and put it on her eyelashes. And Maybelline red lipstick was pretty cheap. She bought some Blue Waltz cologne from the dime store. It was about ten or twelve cents.

"She liked to put on the makeup, and she usually wore some kind of clean apron. She always hurried to get her hair out of pin curls and a turban by the time Daddy got home, but she didn't always succeed. Those times, Dad would tell her how ugly she was. He said she had a big hooked nose. He said she was fat.

"I didn't think my mom was so ugly and fat. And as much as I looked at her, I couldn't see that she had 'a big hooked nose.' But I started to think that maybe she should make herself prettier so Daddy wouldn't get so mad. I started to think that she was causing the fights by looking so ugly.

"She didn't have much time to fix up, what with all the things she had to do, but she tried to brush her hair and put makeup on before Daddy got home. Besides telling her that she was fat, Daddy used to tell her that her skin was the color of urine. Can I say that word?"

"It's okay, just this once," I said.

"Her skin was a yellow urine color, and her hair matched it. Was that okay, you sure?"

"It's okay. Don't worry."

"Dad's sisters were really skinny and had no kids at that time. Dad would tell my mom to try to dress like them, to wear shorts. One time, when she did wear shorts, he laughed at her and said things like, 'Cover yourself up. You make me puke just looking at you. Can't you cover up those purple veins in your legs? And can't you do anything about your big flabby belly? I'm ashamed of you. My sisters all laugh at you, you're so ugly.'

"But I don't think they were really laughing at her. They lived downstairs and next door. When I would hear things they said, they never said any bad things about Mommy. They always asked me how she was and things like that. Even when they talked with Grandma, they didn't say anything bad at all about Mommy. But she always thought they didn't like her.

"I once asked Mommy how come she was so fat all the time. I think she started crying, so I felt bad about asking. Maybe she wasn't fat. I don't know. She never sat down at the table to eat. I don't know how she got so fat. I never saw her eat hardly anything, but her stomach was always sticking out a lot.

"And there were times when she left. A couple of days later, she'd come back with a baby. One time it was Jack. Another time it was Martha. And then she brought Erik home. My dad was pretty mad about her bringing home all those babies. He said this had to stop.

"I didn't know where they were coming from. Well, at least I didn't then. But it's been a long, long time, and I've been listening. I can hear things from way down here. I've been real quiet, well, at least before you came here. I think I know more things now than I did then. Like, I think I know that boys and girls are different.

"It's a funny thing. I couldn't figure out why my brother could go to the bathroom standing up and I couldn't. So, my mom said I had to learn it. She told me to go ahead and try. I did, but when I tried, it was very messy. Mommy laughed. I secretly tried it a few more times, but I never got any better at it. I just figured it was something I'd never learn to do.

"Mommy told me things that got me really mixed up. One time, she told me I would grow up to be a horse. One time, I asked where babies came from, and she said from hot dogs. So, I took a hot dog, wrapped it up in a little warm piece of flannel rag, and hid it in my dresser drawer.

But it never turned into a baby. And she got really mad when she found it in my dresser drawer. It was all old and smelly. I guess you know that it didn't turn into a baby. I don't think I'm so dumb anymore, well maybe a little but not a real lot. Like I said, I've been listening, you know. But still, there are some things that have me confused."

She looked off into the distance for a while and quickly whipped her head back as if to shake a thought away.

"So, do you still want me to tell you more stuff I know about everything?" she asked me. "You have to know everything, even the small stuff. That way, you'll understand. You'll understand it all."

"Yes! Most definitely, I want to hear everything." I thought that if I stayed with her longer, then she would lead me to the terrible girl I was looking for.

"Okay, even if you don't want to listen, please, promise you'll try, please? I've been waiting so long to tell. For so long, I didn't say anything. I tried to be good all this time and not say anything, but I can't anymore. I just got to say it all."

"Okay, I promise."

"But what if it's not important to you?" she asked.

"Oh, but it is! It all is. Please, go ahead."

"Okay, but tell me if you want me to stop, okay?"

"I will."

"Mommy would make her own soap most times. It was lye soap. She would boil something on the stove, take it out, and dry it on strings. I don't remember all the steps, but it had a really bad smell. You could hardly breathe it. Her hands got really red and cracked after making it. But real soap cost a lot of money, and Mommy was always trying to save money. She used the lye soap for scrubbing the floor and washing clothes.

"Sometimes, we had Ivory soap, 'the soap that floats,' to wash ourselves with, but when we ran out of that, we'd use a little of the lye soap. But we had to rinse it off right away because, otherwise, it would burn us really bad.

"We had a clothes washer with a tub and a wringer attached. She would roll that into the bathroom and do our wash. Each piece of clothing had to be carefully pushed through the wringer and into a basket. One time, she got her fingers caught. She was able to get them out, but they were red and swollen. I think it really must have hurt, but she just kept on washing. When Daddy found out, he laughed and said that women were always getting their bits in a wringer, that they couldn't do anything right.

"After the clothes were wrung out, Mommy would hang each piece out on the clothesline. We lived on the second floor, and there was a pulley line attached to the garage below. The pulley line was really squeaky. Now, from down here, I sometimes hear blue jays. Every time I hear one, it sounds just like that old pulley line.

"The clothes smelled really good when they were dry and ready to be ironed. I liked it when Mommy let me sprinkle them before she ironed them. We had a little plastic bottle that had a sprinkler top and a cork on the bottom so you could fit it into any bottle. I got to sprinkle the clothes, and then Mommy would roll them up, ready to be ironed. Mommy said if she couldn't iron them right away, that she would have to put them in the icebox until she was ready to do the ironing. Otherwise, they'd get moldy. She ironed clothes and cleaned the house. She was always cleaning or cooking or washing.

"Lots of times, my daddy would come home from work complaining that his back hurt. He had this salve, Capsolene, and Mommy would rub his back with it. But her hands were always dry and she had cracked skin, sometimes even cuts, and the salve got in the cuts and burned her hands so much that she'd cry. If she couldn't do it, then Daddy would make one of my older sisters Helen or Sadie rub his back with that Capsolene. But it stayed on their hands a long time, and they had to be careful about getting it near their eyes or nose. If they did, then it would burn them real bad.

"Other times when he came home from work complaining about his back, he would take a hot bath. Helen, Sadie, or I would have to go in and wash his back. We really didn't like to do that ... just because, well, we didn't like it.

"Most days after supper, Dad would open a quart of beer, Hamm's or Pabst. I don't think he liked Schlitz or some other one. He complained that it gave him heartburn or something. He'd sit at his desk doing paperwork. By the time he was on the second quart, he would start mumbling again about how hard he worked and how much money was being spent, complaining that Mom was stealing his money. He'd pound the desk and go wild. He'd yell that she'd stolen from his wallet. Every night, he counted his money, wrote the amount on a slip of paper, and slept with his wallet under his pillow.

"I couldn't quite understand the money problems because, at night when he was by his desk, he'd always have a big roll of dollars to count. Lots of them I saw, had 'twenty' or 'fifty' written on them, and I knew that was a lot.

"Most of our clothes and toys we got from other people who outgrew them. One time, my teacher gave me a box of clothes.

"One day, Mommy had no money, and there was no food in the house. She begged Daddy for money for groceries, but he said no, she'd have to wait. She went down to ask Grandma to lend her some, but Grandma said she didn't have any. We needed food for supper and lunches.

"Mommy decided to get out the shopping cart, take all the empty beer bottles back, and get the deposits back so she could buy us some food. Daddy always had lots of empty beer bottles.

"I think it was Jack and I who helped her load them all into the shopping cart and then we walked a long ways to the beer store. We had food that night. After supper, my dad asked where she had gotten the money for the food, because that morning she told him she didn't have any money. He yelled really loud and pounded on the table when he found out she'd used his beer bottle deposit money for food. He said it was his money and she had stolen it. He said he wouldn't give her money for food for a week. He said she already stole enough from him by taking the bottles back for the deposits. He wrote down an amount and told her she'd have to pay him back.

"He wanted to know who had helped her take the bottles back. When he found out it was me and Jack, he went to the pantry. We all knew what he was looking for: the pitta. We were all scared when he took out the pitta. The pitta was a beating stick. I don't know why we called it a pitta. I never heard anyone else ever say that word. But the pitta was made out of an old axe handle that had a double layer of pointy leather strips about eighteen inches long screwed to the end. One time, I counted six on each side. It had a hanging strip on one end so Daddy could put it on a hook in the pantry so that it was always ready when needed. He took out the pitta and pulled our pants down and then gave me and my little brother a beating for helping Mommy with the beer bottles.

"He didn't usually spank us with his hands, not if he could find the pitta. He'd take our pants down to bare skin, grab one arm, and beat us with the leather strips at least six times. If you tried to cover your butt with your free hand, you'd get an extra hit.

"Sometimes, we would hide the pitta. But when he couldn't find it, he'd take his belt off and fold it in half to hit us with that. Sometimes, if he had a shoe handy, he'd use that. But he said the shoe was too soft and we deserved the belt or the pitta, as those hurt more. At least two or three times, he slipped and whacked us with the belt buckle, too. I don't remember which was worse, the belt or the pitta.

"That day, my mom got a punishment, too. Daddy was so mad at her that he took her lipstick and crunched it up in the toilet. He dumped her powder out along with her mascara. He went to the bathroom on them. He broke up her little rouge containers and made sure they got flushed down the toilet, too. Then, he yelled at her. He laughed and told her that everyone would see how bad she looked without any makeup.

"I snuck to the bathroom to see if I could pull anything out. I remember seeing all the lipstick squashed on the sides in the toilet bowl. The mascara was crushed and melting at the bottom of the bowl. None of it could be saved. I thought the toilet would overflow, but it didn't. I felt really sad for Mommy. That night, I cried myself to sleep.

"My mom was really sad and cried most of the time Daddy was at work. She would sing us a song I can remember. It was a song I think she made up. I don't know. I never heard anyone else sing it, and I never heard it on the radio."

The little girl tried to sing with an off-key, hoarse voice:

Please mister, take me in your car.
I want to see my mommy.
They say she lives in heaven.
Is it very far away?
I'm a poor little beggar girl.
My mommy, she is dead.
My daddy is a drunkard man.
He won't give me no bread.
As I sit by the window and hear the organ play,
Oh God, bless my mommy, for she is far away.

I knew the song. I remembered it too.

The little girl continued speaking. "Mommy would tell us how one day she would go away and we would never see her again. She said she hoped that one day we'd come home from school and find her dead. She'd play sad records and cry. We would all say, 'Please, don't die, Mommy. Please, don't die.' Then we would all cry for a long time. We kept telling her, 'Mommy, don't cry.' But she didn't seem to hear.

"She never raised her voice to my dad. If she asked him for something, she would have to beg. He always yelled at her. No one ever talked back to him. When he came into a room, you stayed quiet and tried not to let him notice you were there. If he noticed you were there and he was in a bad mood, he'd start some kind of trouble with you.

"He was always in control. Everybody listened to him, no matter what. Even if he made fun of you or someone else, even Mommy, you had to laugh. Daddy was always the center of attention. I started to learn that that was the way grownups acted. I could learn to be loud and also learn the swearwords, and then people would listen to me. But I wouldn't be mean like him. I'd just be loud and make fun of people and stuff.

"I didn't want to end up sad like my mommy. I didn't want to cry all day. Though I felt real bad for her, I couldn't understand why she never yelled back at him, especially when she knew he was wrong. I didn't want to be like that, always sad, always sad.

"Sometimes, if we were in the car and we passed a wedding, my dad would yell out the window, 'You're crazy! You'll be sorry!' or 'Get rid of her now before it's too late!'—or 'She's a pig!' if the bride looked ugly. We'd all laugh and yell out the window, 'You're crazy,' too. One time we yelled, 'She's a pig!' but we got in trouble because my dad said that the bride was pretty."

Fun Times

"Things couldn't have been all that bad all the time. Now really, you must have had some fun, some good times. Everyone has some fun, at least sometime!" I said.

"There were some fun times, yes, but, as fun as they were, by the end of the day, they'd always turn bad."

"Tell me about the fun times. This is what I want to hear."

"There were some fun times. There were some ..." The girl looked into the distance, searching for her thoughts. "Christmas, I used to look forward to it. We all looked forward to it."

"Yes, yes. Tell me about Christmas!"

"Well, first we'd go out to buy a tree. It was especially fun if there was snow outside. We would go with Daddy to different places to get the best tree. Then, we'd bring it home and put it in a bucket filled with sand. Daddy had to tie it to the walls at the top so it wouldn't fall over.

"Then, we'd get the lights out of the old Christmas boxes in the attic. There were plain colored lights, lights with tinfoil stars around them, and lights that looked like candles with bubbles coming up inside the glass. Some of the light strings were really old. When you plugged them in, all the lights in the house would shut off. Daddy said we blew a fuse. When that happened, Daddy would put a penny or a piece of tinfoil around the fuse and screw it back in. But we couldn't leave the tree lit too long because Daddy said it could cause a fire.

"Mommy loved to decorate. She always put a really pretty Nativity scene under the tree. It was a cardboard manger with hay and cows painted on the back. On the side, there was a music box that had a key sticking out so you could wind it up and hear it play 'Silent Night.' There was a hole at the top in the back where you could put in a light, and Mommy always put a blue light in there. There was Mary, Joseph, and baby Jesus. She also put camels, wise men, and shepherds—and lots of sheep. She had some cotton with glitter on it to make it look like snow."

"It was so beautiful! I liked to imagine I was there," I said.

"She'd also make a little village with houses that had pretend snow on them. Then, she'd put some tiny ice-skater people on a blue mirror so it would look like real ice. There were tiny trees with frosted snow and Santa with his sled filled with tiny presents and reindeer. Rudolph was the leader, and he would always stand in front. All around the village, she put a little white fence. And when Daddy could make the train set work—sometimes, the transformer would burn out—a little train would run around the whole thing. All the relatives would come over on Christmas Eve, and Santa Claus would come over, too, and give us gifts.

"But for weeks before Christmas, Mommy and Daddy would fight. Daddy never wanted to give Mommy any money. He didn't want to buy anyone gifts. He said we all cost too much money and the gifts were the food and clothes he gave us all year long. Fight, fight, fight! I remember he told her to crawl on her belly like a snake if she wanted money for gifts. He really did make her get down on the floor. But she couldn't crawl on her stomach. Sometimes, her stomach was too fat to crawl on, so she just got on the floor. Then, he would throw the money at her and laugh. He would yell and fight every day right up to Christmas Eve.

"I remember Mommy saying that her back hurt. I felt bad that Daddy wanted her to crawl on her stomach because I thought that would make her feel worse. But she never made us rub her back with Capsolene or wash her back in the tub.

"As soon as the people came over on Christmas Eve, Daddy was very friendly. He was the most important person at the party. He would sing songs with everyone and tell jokes. Everyone was kissing and hugging. Every Christmas Eve gave me hope that the fights and the yelling were over forever.

"But the next day, he'd just stay in bed and complain about all the money he had spent. He never opened the gifts we made him until days later. Then he just kind of threw them aside. No matter what we gave him, he just didn't like it. It seemed like he always wanted something bigger or better and that we never gave him enough. Then, he'd say it was all his money, anyway. If he was going to buy himself a gift, he wouldn't waste money on garbage like what we had gotten for him.

"Our gifts were always a disappointment to him. Sometimes, we would make him a craft. Then, he would complain and say, 'What am I supposed to do with this?'

"Lots of our aunts and uncles would give us envelopes that had a Christmas card with money inside for us to buy a present for ourselves. Whenever that happened, Daddy would take the money and say that it was for the presents he had to buy for us and also to cover the cost of the food for the party.

"Soon, I learned not to ask for any toys or dolls for Christmas. I pretty much felt I was just causing trouble asking for anything but money."

"But that couldn't have been every Christmas. Surely, there were other fun things that you did?" I said.

"Yeah, it was every Christmas, every Christmas I can remember. Even the one that was supposed to be special wasn't. My Uncle Bobby was in the Marines. He was my godfather. He came to see us at Christmas when he got back from Japan. He brought me an orange silk kimono from Japan, a real one. Mommy said it was too good for me to wear, so she said she'd keep it for me. But I don't remember ever seeing it again.

"That Christmas turned out bad, too. I think my dad punched Uncle Bobby. By the end of the night, the yelling was so loud that the police came over. Anyway, that was how Christmas was usually celebrated."

"Okay, aside from Christmas, did you have some fun somewhere?" I asked.

"I guess so, if I think real hard. Some other things would start out to be fun, too. I remember we used to save Bowman milk caps. About once a summer, we'd use them to go to the kiddie park. There were a couple of kiddie parks then. One of the best was Kiddieland. They had ponies there. The pony rides cost the most Bowman caps, so only one or two of us could ride them.

39

"One time, as we were coming back from Kiddieland, Daddy was holding my hand to go up the back stairs. Somehow, he slipped and let go of my hand, and I fell down the stairs. We had to go to the hospital and get my arm in a cast.

"I always felt that he kind of let go of my hand on purpose. But no one ever said anything, and I didn't know for sure why I even thought that. But one night after that, while I was still awake in bed, I thought I heard him say something like, 'Should've pushed a little harder so she'd break more than her arm.' But I don't really think I want to remember that part.

"Sometimes, we'd have birthday parties. If we did, all the aunts and uncles came over to celebrate. They gave us cards with money to buy presents. My dad took the money. He said it was to pay for the party and the cake.

"The birthday parties usually ended up with card games the adults played for money. There was always a pile of coins in the middle of the table. They'd drink and smoke. Sometimes, money would fall through the crack in the center of the table and onto the floor. After the parties, early in the morning me and Jack would crawl under the table to see if we could find some dimes or quarters. Most times, if Daddy saw us pick up any coins, he said they were his.

"In second grade, I had a First Communion party. That's when I got this Jesus statue." She proudly held up the statue for me to see. "Lots of people gave me cards with money, but my dad took all of it because he said the cake cost so much. He took the silver dollar my grandfather gave me for my First Communion. He said he would give me a paper dollar in exchange, but he never did.

"Sometimes, the family would visit my grandma and grandpa, my mother's mom and dad, who lived about sixty miles away. I know it was sixty miles because my dad always complained, 'I have to drive sixty miles into the country after driving all week in the truck.'

"But all of us kids looked forward to those times. Sometimes, we would all stay overnight. The next morning, we'd blow up the pool and play in the water. If Daddy was feeling like it, he'd take us to the beach.

"But Mommy warned us not to ask him to take us to the beach. She was always afraid that he wouldn't watch us and we'd drown. Sometimes, he'd drink beer at the beach, flirt with girls, and forget we were there. Those times, he didn't really watch us.

"Sometimes, it was really hot. I would forget what Mommy told us and would ask Daddy to take us to the beach. But when he got back, Mommy would be really mad at us for being so bad. And she'd be mad at him, too. So, even if it was fun at the time, we were in trouble the rest of the day once we got back.

"Although I tried to be good, I was bad at most everything. Before I went to bed I'd always ask Mommy if I was bad or good. Her answer was always the same: I was bad. Most times, there would be a big fight on the way home from Grandma's house. Not just about the beach thing, but about all kinds of things, like what Grandma said or what Daddy said or what Mommy or her sister said—or the regular money thing. Anyway, no matter what it was that started the fight, it always ended with the money thing.

"On the way home, Daddy would drive on the wrong side of the road and say he was going to kill us all. The other cars were headed straight for us, and we were all screaming. Then, at the last minute, he'd switch lanes and get back in the right lane. Or else he would say he was going to drive into a tree. He would drive the car real fast a little off the road and head toward a big tree. When we couldn't scream any louder, he would get back on the road before he hit the tree. Then he would laugh at us and make fun of our screaming. Sometimes, he'd try to hit Mommy with one hand while he was driving, but he couldn't always reach because she'd move over.

"Sometimes, Dad would reach over to try to pull the earrings out of her ears. She had pierced ears, and we were all worried how much that could hurt. We tried to reach over the car seat to come in between him and her earrings, but sometimes, we'd get whacked in the face.

"It was really horrible. Sometimes, my mother would faint or pretend to faint. My dad would yell for us to check if she was dead so he could, so he could … so he could …"

"Go on."

"You sure it's okay?"

"Yes, I promise. It's okay."

"Okay. So … so he could go to the bathroom on her. He said he couldn't wait till she was dead so he could, you know also do that on her grave. We were all crying. My mother would be yelling and saying that she was going to jump out of the car. One time, she did, but we were going kind of slow at that time, so she was alright.

"When we got home, I somehow fell down the steps again. I thought I felt someone push me, but I don't really know. Maybe someone backed up by accident. And then I had to go to the hospital with another broken bone, a collarbone or an arm bone. I had to wear a cast for a long time. I don't remember what was broken.

"I had nightmares almost every night. It was like that all the time. You'd hope you were going to have a fun day, but then it would just turn out bad. We were all bad kids, and the fights were always our fault.

"Now I remember! There was another time that we caused a great big fight! And this time, it wasn't just my fault. We were going to North Dakota. I don't remember why. It was supposed to be another fun time. I think we were going to visit a relative there and were going to be staying with them for a couple days. My dad drove all day and night because he didn't want to spend money for a motel just to sleep. He kept saying what a good driver he was to make it that far without any stops. I think it was eight hundred miles or something like that.

"There were all of us kids and Mom and Dad in the car. We all got really hungry, but all we could find was a hamburger place that had carhops come out to the car to take your order. My dad didn't want to have that service because he didn't want to pay a tip, so we parked by the edge and one of us went in to order stuff. I don't know if it was me or my brother who went in to order. Anyway, we got some things wrong. We did try to remember exactly what everyone wanted, but I guess we got some things mixed up.

"When Daddy opened his sandwich, it wasn't what he wanted, so he started yelling at us and trying to hit us in the car. He got so mad that he took all our sandwiches and sodas away and threw them out the window, all over the driveway. He started yelling out the window. People were looking at us. Then, he started speeding away through the car lot. We were crying. Some of us had food in our mouths, and I think my little brother Jack started throwing up. So, we had to wait until we got to the relative's house to eat something.

"My dad was right. My mom and he would probably have never fought if it wasn't for us kids. We used up too much of his money and did everything wrong. Like the time we all went to Kings Park View. We were all bad. Yeah, I think we were all bad."

The little girl paused. A smile came over her face. She turned her head and smiled as if she were seeing the place.

"Kings Park View was like a giant Kiddieland. You'd pay ten cents to get in. Sometimes, kids under ten got in free. We all had to say we were under that age, even my sisters, who were about twelve. But Kings Park View, it was a magical place!"

The little girl's eyes shone as she continued her story.

"You'd enter through a gate, and it sounded and smelled like a party. There were lots of noises, but good noises! No one was fighting. Men shouting, 'Hurry! Hurry! Step right up.' Loud organ music from the merry-go-round filled the air, as did screams from the Ghost Train, and a silly fat lady always laughing. I think her laughing was a record playing, because she did the same laugh over and over: 'ah ha ha ha ha, ah ha ha ha ha', and she always said the ah ha ha in the same tone.

"You could see bright lights, scary rides, and lots of people, people eating big fluffs of pink cotton candy or hot dogs, people holding balloons and prizes, people laughing, and lots of sailors kissing girls.

"Sometimes, you'd see sailors and their girlfriends sitting on a bench and 'mushing.' Jack and I would laugh at them. One time, Jack laughed too loud, and one of the sailors yelled, 'Hey, kid, beat it.' So, we went back to hold our mom's hand while we walked around.

"I turned around and stuck my tongue out at that sailor, but I turned back around right away so Mommy didn't see. Jack saw me do it, and he did the same thing. Then, as we walked, we walked really close to Mommy, but the sailor didn't come after us, so that was good.

"There were so many things to see that we didn't know which way we wanted to go first. We talked about what rides we wanted to go on. We would dare each other to go on the big rides, but we knew we were secretly too scared of them!

"First, you'd see the big wooden tracks of a roller coaster. You could hear the clackety-clack of the cars slowly being pulled up the hill. As they reached the top, the screaming began before the cars zoomed down one big hill and up another. You could feel the ground rumble as the cars passed by. That was too big of a ride for us to go on, but it was fun to watch.

"Right next to it was a big red Tilt-a-Whirl with swirling cars and more screams. There were weight-guessing games where you sat in a chair that was really a scale. There was a man there who tried to guess how much you weighed. If he was wrong, you won a prize.

"And there was another place where we watched strong men hit a hammer to try to ring the bell. Some guys had to try over and over. Lots of Army men and Navy sailors lined up with their girlfriends next to them to try to ring the bell. When one of them rang the bell, his girlfriend would give him a kiss.

'Blech' Jack and I would yell. We said, 'You're crazy!' or 'She's a tramp!' We really didn't know what *tramp* meant, but we heard my daddy say it lots of times, so we figured it was okay to say.

"One time, one of the sailors came over and yelled at us, so we shut up real fast and pretended we didn't know why he was yelling at us.

"Then, we watched lots of adults in line to go into the Tunnel of Love! It was just a ride that had cars that looked like boats floating on the water and then going into a dark tunnel. It didn't look scary or anything. I don't know why there was such a big line to go on such a stupid ride.

"A little farther into the park were the dunk tanks. A dunk tank was where a guy sat in a cage and you threw a baseball at a target next to the cage. If you hit the target, the guy would fall in the water and pretend he was really mad and surprised. It was always a dark man in the dunk tank. We called them colored people. The guys throwing the ball at the target called them something else. It was a bad name. We were not allowed to say it in front of anyone, especially a colored person. The dunk tanks were the only bad area in Kings Park View.

"We watched for a while, but my mom made us move along because a lot of the ball throwers were saying very bad things and getting too loud. Sometimes, a fistfight would break out between the ball throwers. We had to stay away so we didn't get hurt.

"There were lots of booths where you could win prizes. Some booths had a tank filled with water that had floating ducks or fish with numbers underneath them. You'd pay about ten cents to pick up three, and if one had a number on it, you could win the prize that had the same number on it. Some of the prizes were pretty nice, but we never won anything good, just a plastic ring or a charm.

"There was one booth where you could get a wooden fishing pole with a plastic hook and hook a wooden fish that also had a number written under it that told you what prize you won. That booth was always busy with lots of moms and dads and their kids.

"My favorite was one booth that had lots of beautiful dolls wearing satin gowns on its back wall. Two men in the front were holding strings that looked like they were attached to the dolls. I talked my dad into giving me a nickel to pull one string to win that doll. He said that I would never win, that it was all fixed, but he gave me the nickel anyway. I pulled the string and won a plastic magnifying glass charm. It was real junky. I tucked it into my pocket because I was kind of embarrassed that I didn't win the doll. I was sure I would. The guy laughed and yelled, 'Next time, listen to your old man, kid.'

"My favorite thing to watch was the Shoot the Chutes ride. It was a roller coaster that rode up a big hill and zoomed down to splash into a small lake. It was too big and scary for us to ride on. Sometimes, if you stood close, you'd get wet. That was kind of fun.

"The park also had a ride called the Ghost Train, where you got into a car that took you in a dark house where scary things popped up in front of your car. I went on it only once. I was too afraid to go again.

"There was one really wild ride that went around and around. It pressed you against the wall and spun around so fast that you stayed there pressed against the wall until the floor dropped down. It was called the Rotor.

"Toward the end of the park was Aladdin's Castle, a scary maze you walked through. It was dark with some mirrored walls. A lot of scary things popped up. I never actually went through it, but that's what everyone said. At the exit was a spinning barrel you had to walk through to leave. As the women were leaving, there'd be a burst of air from the floor that would blow their dresses up. You could see their underpants. Jack and I would watch and laugh.

"The biggest ride was the parachutes. A really high tower with cables would pull a parachute up. When the top of the parachute hit the top of the tower, it would pop open the parachute and send you plunging to the ground. It seemed too scary to even be a ride. And there always seemed to be one stuck at the top. We didn't go on any of these rides, but they were fun to watch.

"You had to pay separately to go on each ride, and we were allowed only one or two rides. The final ride was the merry-go-round. It was only one ticket each, and we were always happy to ride on it. Some of the horses went up and down. If you were little, you'd need to someone to hold onto you so you wouldn't fall off. There weren't too many of those kinds of horses. The merry-go-round went pretty fast, and the horses were slippery. There were plain horses that didn't move, but those were for babies. They also had benches you could sit in, but that was really stupid. Sometimes, old geezers sat there and held babies that were crying. When it was our turn to get on, we all ran to get on the up-and-down horses. My mom was afraid that we might fall off when the horses went up and down.

"That day, my mommy had baby Erik to watch. He was too little to go on the ride. Anyway, he was sleeping in the buggy, so Mommy couldn't go on with us. She made my daddy go on with us and hold us on the horses. After it was over, my dad said it had made him sick and dizzy. He yelled at my mom for making him take us. Everyone was looking at us, and I could see that this was very embarrassing for my mom. Then, still looking back and yelling, Daddy left the park without us."

The happiness left the girl's eyes. She cast them downward and frowned.

"The fun stopped. It was our fault. We'd been bad. We shouldn't have asked to go on the merry-go-round or, at least, not those dangerous up-and-down horses. Mommy was crying. She didn't know what to do. It was dark, and home was about three or four miles away. We all looked and looked, but Dad was nowhere in sight. She even asked someone at the entrance to call him on the big loudspeaker several times. But Daddy didn't show up. It seemed we waited a long time. When Mommy realized that Daddy had really left us and we had to walk home, she started crying really hard. We were all scared.

"We had to cross a big bridge over a river. You could see the water under your feet as you walked across. It was a metal bridge, the kind that opens up. It made me dizzy to look down. Well, Mommy had to cross it with all us kids and the baby in the buggy. There were five of us for her to worry about. The buggy went bumpity-bumpity-bump over the metal bridge. Then, we got to the part where there was a bigger space between the metal grates. It was big enough that one of us could have fallen through. This was the middle that pulled apart and opened up the bridge so that big boats could go under it. We were scared they would open the bridge. Then we saw a bright flash of lightning and heard loud thunder. It started to rain.

"Some of us, maybe me, started screaming. Mommy yelled at us to walk faster. We all held hands. The thunder and the bumpity-bump of the buggy made my baby brother, Erik start to cry. Mommy was still crying, too. Her tears and the raindrops made the black on her eyelashes run down her face. She looked really bad. She'd look down and say she wanted to jump into the black water and end all her troubles. We were all crying and scared when we finally got to the other side. We were worn out and hungry, but we knew that when we got home, we wouldn't eat anything. We'd have to get in bed fast.

"When we got home, Daddy wasn't there. We had to go downstairs and ask Grandma for a key to let us in. We all jumped in bed as quickly as we could. Then, we heard him coming up the back steps. Everyone told each other, 'Please, don't say anything. Don't start any trouble.' Then, we'd beg Mom not to say anything before running back to bed. We all pretended to be fast asleep.

"He came in without saying anything at first. He sat at his desk and started to drink beer. After a couple of bottles, he started talking to himself again about how my mother was stealing all his money. He talked about the money he wasted on rides and stuff for us at Kings Park

View and how he was really sick and dizzy because he had had to hold us on the merry-go-round. Then, he talked about how hard he worked while Mommy just sat home. 'Never worked a day in her life,' he'd say. 'Your mother doesn't know what it means to work!' Then, after he had few more beers, he'd say, 'She's nothing but a hoo-wer.'"

The little girl looked up at me. "It's something bad, isn't it?"

"Yes," I said. "It's something bad."

"I kind of figured it was, but I don't think my mom was a hoo-wer, whatever that means. I don't think she was bad, just sad. Are you mad at me because I said it? I never said it before."

"No, I understand."

"'Cause I just wanted to let you know what he said in case it wasn't a bad thing; then, I could stop thinking it was."

"It's okay, it's okay," I reassured her.

"We all pretended to be asleep so he wouldn't think anyone was listening to him. But he wanted us to hear him, so he came into our bedrooms and yelled for us to wake up. We were all still quiet, but we knew the words would soon come that would force Mom to 'start.' Being quiet didn't help. He just got louder. 'Hey, kids, did you know your mother goes around with a mattress on her back?'

"I remember thinking that must be pretty hard to do because mattresses are so heavy. I thought he was saying how strong she was. I thought she would be happy to hear that. But she wasn't. Maybe she didn't think it was ladylike to be so strong. Maybe he was jealous because he couldn't carry one. I don't know.

"Then he would pull Jack out of bed and make him sit at the desk. He would start to tell him really bad things, like swearing things and bad words about girls. Jack would start crying, but Daddy wouldn't let him leave the chair to go to bed. He just started yelling more bad stuff.

I wanted to save Jack. I wanted to tell Daddy to leave him alone, but I was too little—and I was scared that I would get hit.

"Then, Mommy yelled to Jack to go to bed. Jack tried to get up, but my dad grabbed him and said that it was about time his son learned what a hoo-wer his mother was. Then, Mommy started yelling at Jack. But Jack just started crying.

"Then she came out of the bedroom and 'started.' She screamed, 'Stop it! Stop it!' She set it off. It was her fault for 'starting.' We knew that the fight was just beginning. She should have kept her mouth shut.

"Dad got even louder. 'Yeah, kids, just ask her when I met her.' Then, it got scary. Sometimes, Dad would try to hit her. Then, she would dare him. Then, we all would run into the middle of it and try to stop him. Sometimes, he really did hit her. Sometimes, he'd miss and hit us. No beating over and over like with the pitta though, only one big punch that someone would get if they got in his way.

"There was no sense pretending we were asleep. We were all out of bed screaming for Mom to be quiet and not say anything. Then, she would get really mad and tell him that she would get a deevorss, I think that's the word, and he would be forced to give her money to support us. Then, he would yell that he wouldn't give her a penny. He'd have Grandma kick us out on the street, and Mom'd have to go on ADC, whatever that was. He'd have the state take us kids away from her.

"She said the police would take him to jail. He said he didn't care. He'd be happy to go to jail just so she wouldn't get any of his money. He would start yelling 'Hey you hear that kids, your father is going to jail.' Then he'd start singing real loud 'hallelujah, I'm a bum' over and over until Mommy would start screaming for him to stop. 'Stop it! Stop it!' she'd scream.

Then, he made fun of her by saying he was going to pull her false teeth out and break them. He tried to reach at her face to do that.

"We all felt really sad because Mommy was crying a real lot! I didn't want him to break her teeth. I didn't want her to know that we knew her teeth weren't real. Dad just laughed at her and called her some other bad names. She cried and cried and cried, and so did we. She went back into the bedroom and stayed quiet. All of us ran back into bed and hid under the covers to bite our nails.

"The fights would last all night. My dad would threaten to call my other grandma long distance, sixty miles away, and tell her how he hated her. He'd threaten to call Uncle Jimmy, my mother's older brother, in the middle of the night, too.

"Then he'd start picking on us. He would call my big sister Helen a piece of stink. Then he'd say all us girls were just pieces of stink. I smelled my feet, but they weren't real dirty. I didn't think they were stinking, so I didn't know why he said that.

"After a long time, when she couldn't stand it any longer, Mommy came out of the bedroom again and yelled, 'Oh yeah. I think I'll go down and get your mother and tell her what you did to your own daughter.' That wasn't the first time I'd heard her say that, so I knew this was when the fight was going to get even worse. After that, she ran back into the bedroom so he wouldn't come after her. Then, he really yelled. He wanted to hit her. We tried to push him away. Several of us got a whack, but we felt it was better that we got one instead of Mommy.

"I wondered what she was going to say about what he did to his own daughter. I wondered who it was. I wondered what it was. Unfortunately, I found out later. All the fun from Kings Park View was erased. I wished we had never gone at all.

"I used to pray myself to sleep. I'd hold my breath to stop my breathing but I couldn't hold it long enough to die. I'd think about Jesus and the angels, praying that Jesus would take me up to heaven, away from all this. Finally, when daylight was near, Dad got tired and went to bed. The next day, Mom was as nice as could be. No one was supposed to say anything to my dad about the fight.

"Mom would be 'silent' for a time after their fights, not talking to Daddy for a day or so. After that, the two would talk normal. Dad never said he was sorry or anything. I couldn't understand it. My dad had said so many bad things, but it was still okay!

"The late-night brawls made it impossible to go to school the next day, so we were absent a lot. I missed so much school that the teacher told me I was absent almost as many days as I was present.

"You might think this next story is funny, but it wasn't funny at the time. I was in third grade. In first and second grade, we wore costumes to school on Halloween. For several days, maybe even a week, before Halloween in the third grade, I was absent because of the fights. But on Halloween, Mom made sure I went to school in a costume. They had prizes, good prizes, and I won the last two years because my costume was so funny. Mom always dressed me as Aunt Jemima, the pancake lady. She corked my face black and put pillows in the front and back of an old dress tied with a rope to hold the pillows. I had a big red turbin on my head and a pair of Daddy's old shoes on my feet. Then, she walked me to school and left.

"Well, this time, I was the only one in school with a costume. It seems they decided not to do the costumes anymore, but I didn't know that because I had been absent when that announcement was made. Sooo, I spent the whole day in school with that stupid costume on. I was really humiliated. The kids and the nuns made fun of me. I didn't like the laughing. It really made me feel bad. At first, the pillows kept falling out of my costume. Also, I couldn't go to the bathroom because the dress was so long. And I couldn't wash that stupid cork off my face.

"So, I don't know if that was one of the fun times or not, but all the kids in school thought it was funny. As soon as they saw me, they laughed. So did the teachers. So I guess it was a fun thing. At least no one was yelling at me.

"One thing I know was fun. I liked to make things. My grandpa worked at a factory. He would sometimes bring me a box of knotholes that came out of wood. I loved to make things out of them. I particularly liked to paste a holy card on the knothole and make a hanger on the top. I even made my own paste out of flour and water. I would then go door to door and try to sell the knot holes. I sold them for ten or twenty-five cents each.

"I also made dolls out of clothespins. I painted faces and used yarn for hair. I found some colorful rags and made clothes for the dolls. People liked my clothespin dolls. I made policemen, ballerinas, cowboys, all kinds of doll people. I sold them for about twenty cents each. I was happy to be able to sell my crafts for money.

"I wanted to save the money. I had a dime bank we got from the March of Dimes. You were supposed to fill it with dimes and give it to people who fight polio. But we didn't have any money to give away, so we just kept the bank. When it was full, I think it held five dollars. I kept saving my dimes in there. My bank was almost full.

"My mom found it one day and told me how bad I was to save money and not tell her. She cried. She said she had to suffer to get money from my dad while I was being selfish, saving money all for myself. She said I was just like my father. I didn't want to be mean like my dad, so I told her she could have it. But then she kept crying and saying, 'No, keep it. You're so selfish.' But she finally took my dimes. I knew she was just going to get us food, so I guessed it was okay. I just felt bad because, while I was proud that I earned that money from selling things I had made, all I did was cause trouble. I didn't plan to sell any more stuff after that.

"One time, I entered an art contest and won a set of encyclopedias. But my dad said that they belonged to him because I'd won them in his house. He took charge of them. We had to ask when we wanted to use one. Lots of times, he would just say no, we didn't need to use any."

"Did you like school?" I asked.

"I liked going to school when I did. I was great at religion and spelling and, of course, art. I won spelling bees all the time. I learned about Jesus at school. I liked to go to church. I used to like to go with my grandma to her church. Most times when I went to church with her, she'd also take me with her to see 'the dead one,' whoever that may have been. She said that you didn't have to know the person to stop in and say a prayer. The funeral home was across the street. After Mass, we'd just go in, say a prayer, take a flower to press in our missals, and leave.

"On Easter or Christmas, sometimes, my mom would go to church with us, if she wasn't too busy. If we got there early, we'd usually see an old woman walking around near the altars praying out loud, blessing everyone out loud, and praising and thanking Jesus. She wasn't a nun or anything. She was just a regular person, one who talked really loud. 'Oh, my Jesus, oh thank you, holy Jesus,' she shouted. We'd make fun of her after Mass. Mom said she was a crazy fanatic.

"I made a secret altar in the closet at home. I'd pretend I was a nun and say secret prayers there. But I had to make sure I wouldn't get caught. My mom didn't like me hiding in the closet. She didn't want me to be a fanatic.

"These are all the fun things I remember."

Mom Gets a Job, 1955

The little girl continued her story. She said, "Mom constantly told us that one day she'd go away and never come back. She told us she'd be in that funeral home across the street from the church one day. When Daddy would take the car to the gas station, she used to smell gas fumes and tell us that one day she would keep smelling the gas fumes and just go to sleep and never get up.

"Sometimes, she would close her eyes, and we would all be afraid that something bad had happened. So, we would shake her and yell, 'Mommy, get up! Get up!' Then, she would.

"Daddy was still complaining about money. He told my mother that she had to help out with the bills. He said he was sick of her sitting at home all day doing nothing. She found a job at a factory, the Big Tin Can Company.

"Sometimes, Dad would drive her there and also pick her up. I heard her say that she could take only the third shift, whatever that meant—about four in the afternoon till midnight. One day, my dad took all of us to Mom's workplace to bring her a snack at break time. I remember that she was so happy because the other workers had made her a tin 'crown' out of cans. They said she was queen of the can company. She showed it to us, but we couldn't touch it because it was really sharp and we could get cut. But it was very pretty.

"My dad got out of the car and went in and started a fight with my mom's boss, Victor. I think my dad hit him. Dad yelled, saying that Victor was doing all kinds of things with my mom, all sorts of things I didn't understand.

"She still was allowed to go back to work there, but she told her sister that she was pretty embarrassed. Mom was paid extra for piecework. That meant the more pieces she made, the more money she got. I think she was trying to work hard. One day, she was working too fast, and I think she got mixed up with what was next on the machine. She got two of her fingers cut off in a punch press. I think she stopped working for a while after that.

"She cooked our meals, but we didn't have a lot of money. Most of the food was saved for Dad. We had bread and gravy a lot. Sometimes, we'd have Franco-American spaghetti mixed with scrambled eggs, but we usually didn't ask for seconds because there would be trouble if Dad wanted more food and it wasn't there. I was small, but I was always hungry.

"One day, the milkman was late getting to our house. Dad stopped back home as the milkman was bringing in the last gallon for my mom. My dad started yelling at him and saying that my mom was secretly doing things with the milkman, the same things he said she had been doing with her boss, Victor. I couldn't figure out what she could be doing with the milkman.

"Poor Mr. Magnus, I think my dad may have hit him. I know that he was yelling back at my dad. Mom was already crying. One of the gallons of milk had broken. There was glass and milk all over the floor. Well, my dad didn't give her money for more milk because he said it was her fault for doing stuff with the milkman. We stopped milk delivery after that. Mommy had to walk to the store whenever she needed milk and the gallons were really heavy to carry.

One time, we ordered from the Home Juice Company. Daddy liked that juice. He was the only one who was allowed to drink the orange juice and blackberry juice. And he would know if we took any, because he'd mark the bottle. Then, he began accusing my mom of doing things with the Home Juice deliveryman. He was yelling something about a slot. But the containers were glass and they didn't have any slots on them. I thought that maybe he was mad because the juice might be running out of an open slot. I don't know how he put it, but he brought up the mattress thing again. We never ordered from Home Juice again.

"Then there was Harold Kwal. He was a nice old man who went door to door selling towels and curtains and drapes. He'd let you buy them on time payments. After my mom picked out some curtains, Harry would come over once a week to get a payment. I think it was a dollar or two. But then, my dad said that we didn't need any fancy curtains or drapes and she was a spendthrift, so he lowered her food 'pay.' That made it impossible for Mom to pay Harry on time. So, sometimes when Harry came to the door, she made us hide and be quiet. We pretended no one was home. I guess she finally paid him off, but not before my dad started yelling and threatening him if he ever came back to our house. My dad raised his hands and tried to hit him, but Harry ducked. Harry never came back.

"After a while, my mom started getting more and more aggravated with us kids. We were too loud, too lazy, and too stupid. It seemed that nothing we did was right. If we got into fights with our brothers or sisters, or if we didn't listen to her, she'd threaten to tell Dad. And she did, all the time. I hated to hear him coming home knowing that at least one us was going to get beat up. And if it wasn't fair and one of us tried to stick up for the other one, then he or she would get a beating, too.

"By the time there were six of us, we all had nicknames. Some of us had more than one. We were fat butt, lard butt, satchel butt, pooper, mental case, Johnny-wet-your-pants, Johnny-high-pockets, bardahl, and falspar. All us girls were pieces of stink. I didn't know why he called us that. Mommy always gave us baths. And I didn't think any of our butts looked like a container of lard or satchels. I think that's a suitcase, isn't it?"

"Sort of," I said.

"How could a butt look like a suitcase? Oh well.

"My dad also made up a song about Sadie: 'Sadie is so fat, she could even eat my hat.' And it was okay to call Helen 'satchel butt.' Daddy loved to sing the 'eat my hat' song. Sadie didn't like it and sometimes she cried, but didn't care. Daddy liked it, and that was all that mattered.

"And some of the nicknames I just didn't understand, like falspar. But we were allowed to call each other those names. Everyone else would always laugh, especially Daddy. And we wanted to see him happy. That way, he wouldn't think to hit us.

J.ROSE GIBSON

"My mom didn't usually hit us, but sometimes she did. Sometimes, she hit us on the butt with a pot or a pan, but that didn't really hurt much. It was almost funny because it made such a whomping sound. But we didn't dare laugh or else she'd take off her shoe to hit us more.

"She never hit us with the pitta. Lots of times, she would threaten to bash our heads against the wall, but she never did that, either. Sometimes, when she was really upset, she'd bang her head against the wall and then sometimes take a handful of aspirins. That would always scare us.

"Often, if we did something wrong, my mom would take our huge box of toys: tiny dolls, army guys, cars, and blocks and throw it all over the floor. Some of our toys would break but we couldn't say anything. We had to pick up each item and then she'd dump the box out again. When that wasn't enough, she would pull out all the pots and pans and throw them all over the floor. The noise was loud and scary. It made me cry. Then, we had to pick them up over and over.

"Many times, my dad hid his wallet downstairs by Grandma because, he said, Mommy would steal his money. One time, when I was downstairs by Grandma, I remember her asking me if I was going to grow up to be like my mother. She told me not to be like my mother, who was lazy and took my dad's money. She said that my mother was a spendthrift and didn't do anything all day but spend my dad's money on herself.

"But even then, I knew that Grandma didn't know the truth. I knew my dad was saying bad things about Mommy to his mother. I saw my mom work really hard cleaning and cooking. I wanted to tell my grandma that she was wrong. I wanted to tell her how hard my mom worked and all. I wanted to tell her all the bad words my daddy was saying. But I didn't because I didn't want to cause any trouble. I felt sorry for my mom. I knew that it would hurt her feelings if she knew that Grandma said that stuff, so I never told her.

"Mom wore really cheap clothes. She never went to Sears or Robert Hall or any fancy place like that. She bought her aprons at the dime store. The only time she spent money for herself was at Bernice's Beauty Shop to get a permanent. Mom dyed her own hair with henna rinse at home. I liked to go with her to the beauty shop because Bernice would give me a pole with a magnet attached that I could push around the floor and use to pick up bobby pins. We went there only a couple times a year. But it didn't really help Mom look pretty. Dad still made fun of her.

"Sometimes, if Mom had an extra dollar, she'd get us a toy at the dime store. I usually chose something for my dollhouse. Sometimes, we'd get a paddleball or some Chinese handcuffs or a yo-yo because they were cheap. They had yo-yos that glow in the dark, you know. But I don't remember too many times that we were able to get toys.

"It was getting difficult for Mom to do all her errands by walking. She was pretty fat again. She said her legs were hurting. The stores were pretty far apart; sometimes, she'd have to go a long way to each one. So, she said she needed to learn how to drive. Daddy laughed and said that she was too old and stupid to learn to drive. He said he wouldn't teach her or pay anyone to teach her. He said she should go out and try to find someone who would teach her for free and he laughed.

"One day my mom was talking to her sister, my auntie Tina, and asked her how she'd learned to drive. Auntie Tina said that she would ask her friend Carl, the man who had taught her how to drive, if he'd be willing to teach my mom. Carl said that he would. He didn't charge my mom anything because he was friends with Auntie Tina. Daddy said it was okay but told my mom to make sure that 'Old Carl' knew he wouldn't get one red cent from Daddy. Carl came over in the evening a couple of times a week to give Mom lessons. He would beep the horn in front of the house to let her know he was there. I remember that Carl was kind of tall and had white hair. He always opened the door for Mommy to get into his car. I was only in fourth grade. Helen and Sadie were in seventh and eighth. They were not old enough to babysit all of us, so Daddy was home with us during those times. We would all watch out the window as Mommy went down the stairs to get into the car. One day, I heard my dad mumble something about how he would have to put an end to this.

"Mom was pretty happy with herself for being able to learn to drive. She looked forward to her lessons. It was okay for a while, but my dad started accusing her of doing something bad with the Carl in the car. He said she must be paying him some way. That ended in a big argument.

I think that by that time, though, my mom had learned enough about driving and was able to drive on her own. So, I never saw Carl come back after that.

"Daddy complained a lot that he was sick. He always thought that something was wrong with him. He said he was working too hard and the kids made him too nervous. Almost every day, he'd make us all take turns rubbing his back with the hot salve or scrubbing his back in the tub.

"My dad was always complaining of 'the shakes,' but I never knew what the shakes were. He thought he had heart trouble or cancer. It was good that my mom learned to drive, because he made my mom take him to the hospital a lot. I don't remember how often he went there, but it seemed like a lot of times. My mom was afraid to drive that far. But the hospital guys always sent Daddy home, saying that there was nothing wrong with him. My sisters and I took home a couple of little green teapots that we got from the canteen at the hospital. I think we really stole them, but I'm not sure. Maybe they were just old and ready to be thrown away, anyway. I remembered liking to play tea party with those little green teapots.

"Each time Dad would come home, he would start talking about money. All the money he made from his trucking business, he kept in his own account. I remember the bank name, Main Bank. Mom never knew how much money he had. He gave his mother more money to save for him, saying that he couldn't trust my mom around money and he didn't want her to know what he had. He kept saying over and over that we needed more money. He got an idea that we could make more money if we took in a boarder. He said his mother ran a boarding house when he was little and there was no reason why my mother couldn't do the same.

"My dad rented out the front bedroom to a boarder for a while, collecting money from him. My dad didn't give my mom more money for food for the boarder, but he told the boarder that meals were included in the price of the room.

"Mommy complained about that because the boarder ate a lot and there was not much left for us kids. By that time, there were six of us kids in the little upstairs apartment. We were running out of space. Our flat, upstairs from Grandma's, had four bedrooms, but the little one in front was reserved for the boarder.

"I don't remember much about the boarder. He'd just walk in and sit down to eat or else go to his room. It was like a stranger was in our house. We couldn't even watch TV when we wanted. We had to be quiet. I didn't like the boarder. But it didn't matter what I liked or not. I never said anything about it or caused any trouble.

"Dad kept stashing his money. He reminded me of a squirrel burying little nuts. Sometimes, I'd see him putting rolls of money wrapped in rubber bands between the mattresses or inside a blue metal box, locking it up and then putting the key in his pocket.

"Sometimes, one of us would get a toothache. We hardly ever went to the dentist. Only when we had a big problem would he take us—and then he would complain the whole time. If we had a toothache, he'd let the dentist drill our teeth. But if we needed braces or had a big problem, then my dad told the dentist to just pull the tooth out.

"My sister Sadie had some teeth pulled out in eighth grade because my dad said it was cheaper than braces. Plus, he said that he had to have his teeth pulled out because of us kids, so we should have ours pulled, too. He said he never had time to go to a dentist because he was working so hard to make money for all of us.

"I remember going to the dentist once or twice. Dad would hold our hands when crossing the street. Whenever he did that, he would crunch our hands back and forth so bad that it hurt. None of us wanted to hold his hand when crossing the street. I would have rather let a streetcar hit me.

"Then, around 1956—I know it was around that time, because I was in the beginning of fifth grade—Mom started talking about their buying a house of their own. My dad didn't like that idea. He said that they were saving money by living in Grandma's house for free. My mom said she had saved up some money by working and that that should help, but the more she saved on food, the less money Dad would give her. He said that if she could afford to save the money, then that proved he was giving her too much for food. Mom started complaining about looking at four walls all day and having no privacy, especially with the boarder.

Dad would then take us out for Sunday drives so she could get free of the four walls.

"On Sundays, we'd drive down Fourth Street and watch the bums panhandle and stumble around. Sometimes, we'd see women all dressed up and walking around alone. My dad whistled at some of the prettier ones and yelled, 'You tramp!' to some of the worst-looking ones. Sometimes, he'd yell out the bad word at the colored people. But we weren't really allowed to say that.

"We saw lots of colored people. Daddy said they were bad and didn't like us. My mom and dad told us to roll up the windows as we drove by a dark person, because he or she might try to take one of us out of the car. I remember asking why, but I don't recall the answer. I think I really do but don't want to remember.

"What I do remember was having lots of nightmares about some colored people being in my house and trying to find me to take me away. But I was usually hiding under the bed.

"The city was building an expressway in those days. Many houses were vacant, ready for demolition. Sometimes, my dad would drive us around and send us through those houses to look for anything left behind. None of the houses were locked. Some had no floors. We didn't go into the houses with no floors or the ones that had walls broken down because they were dangerous places. But in others, we found a lot of good stuff—furniture, clothes, records. Some stuff was junk, but we took it anyway. We could always find some use for it or else sell it at Paul's Coal Shop.

"Mom and Dad, mostly Mom, were still talking about buying a house. We went in lots of different open houses. Most times, we kids had to stay in the car because, Dad said, if they saw how many kids he had, they wouldn't sell him the house. One house was near the area where the new expressway was to be built. It cost fourteen thousand. It was big. It had four bedrooms and a kitchen and a front room and a big basement with a great big coal furnace that almost filled up the whole basement.

"My dad and mom talked a lot about it, but my dad wasn't in favor of buying a house. He didn't like the idea of the coal furnace and all the work it took to make the house warm in the winter. He also said he wouldn't be able to shovel the snow, work around the house, and still keep up his job. My mother promised that she would shovel the coal into the furnace every morning before anyone was awake, making sure it was warm. She also promised to shovel the snow and rake the leaves. But Dad still hesitated. After a few days, my mom called the real estate agent and asked if the house was still for sale. He told her that someone else wanted to buy it. She begged him to let her and my dad have the first chance. He said okay, but only if she would give him a deposit that day. She borrowed some money from either the aunties or Grandma. I got on the streetcar with her to take that ten-dollar deposit to hold the house. The agent promised to give it back the next day if my mom couldn't convince my dad to buy the house.

"Well, there was another big fight that night, but Mom convinced Dad that we needed to move. This was the only fight that I remember where she got what she wanted.

"She promised she would go to work again. And she did. Before we left grandma's upstairs flat, Mom went to work again at the Big Tin Can Company. She gave all her money to Dad to buy the house. She worked hard from four to midnight, but she always managed to make us lunches and get supper ready. Our lunches were mostly egg sandwiches. Dad always got a hot lunch and a breakfast with sausage or bacon, eggs, and toast."

The little girl stood up and stretched. She was taller than I thought.

"So, now you know. You don't have to look any farther. I'm the bad girl you knew. I was bad most of the time. I know you came here to find out why Jesus took your boy. It was probably my fault. I know. I caused a lot of trouble, and I always did bad things. Are you going to hurt me now?"

"No, I wouldn't hurt you—and you weren't bad. But there's more to tell me, isn't there?" I said.

"But I was bad. Everybody told me I was bad."

"But so far, I don't think you were bad. Maybe if you tell me more. Maybe there is something terrible you did and you're not telling me. Did you ever, well, did you ever hurt someone real bad or make them, well, die?"

The little girl turned her head and stopped abruptly.

"I'll tell you more, but, please, promise that you won't hit me or leave me here."

"I won't. I won't leave you here, and I won't hit you!"

"Promise?"

"Yes, I promise."

"I'm scared to tell more. You might not want to know."

"But you have to, you know?"

"I know. I guess I always knew I'd have to tell."

She was silent for a while, deciding what to do. Then, she said, "Okay, but it's not my fault if you get mad."

"Agreed," I said.

The Big House, 1957

"We moved to the house. It was big. Mom kept her promise about the furnace, sometimes shoveling the coal before it was light outside. I could hear her from upstairs when I was still in bed. She also kept her promise about shoveling the snow and raking the leaves.

I was in sixth grade. By that time, I'd learned to believe the worst of everybody. Dad especially liked his kids to make each other jealous. We were always given his approval when we made fun of each other.

I tried to walk straight. Lots of times, Dad would make fun and say, 'What are you doing, pushing out your mosquito bites for someone to grab?' or something like that. Then, he would pinch my chest and laugh. I hated that, so I kind of scrunched my shoulders down a lot and walked stooped over so nobody else would notice me. Pretty soon, I got a little bra, but that didn't stop my dad from pinching my chest or laughing at me.

"My brothers and sisters and I didn't talk much to each other or have secrets. One of us would always be delighted to get the other in trouble by telling Dad or Mom. Whoever snitched on the other was treated nicely and could be assured that Daddy would pay attention to his or her every word. If we didn't tell on each other, then we'd get a beating. So, we were always eager to be the first to tell Dad which one of us had been bad. We were taught that if people were nice to us, it was because they wanted something from us.

"I learned early that it was a good thing to lie, because everyone lied. No one really meant what they said, so you could say just about anything. I learned that if people were rich, they laughed at you. If they were poor, they were looking for a handout. If they asked how you were, they were just being nosy.

"I learned that it was a good idea to be nice to people who were rich and to look pathetic in front of them, because they might give you some money if they liked you or felt sorry for you. 'Those are the kind of people you want to know. Those are the people you treat right,' Dad would say. We were also told that no one liked any of us. If they acted like they did, then they were just secretly making fun of us.

"At first, I thought I could grow up to be a piano player or a singer, teacher, artist, ballerina, scuba diver—even a swimmer like Esther Williams. But I soon learned that I couldn't be any of these, nor could any of my brothers and sisters. We learned that all of us were too dumb to do any of those things. Those things were for the special people, not us.

"I wanted to learn Polish or French, but my mom and dad told me that anyone who wanted to learn another language was just being phony, trying to make people think they were someone they weren't.

"We weren't allowed to take swimming lessons because my mom thought that if we did, we'd actually think we could swim and would then jump into the lake and drown. She said that it would be a waste to take lessons because we would never learn to swim no matter how many lessons we took.

"One day, I told my mom that my friend Gina was going to be a lawyer. I asked her why I couldn't be one, too. She said it was because Gina was different. 'Look at her and look at you. Those things are for other girls to do, not you. You'll be lucky if you find someone who'll marry you. You should just plan to look for a job right now and then find someone to marry you.'

"I was still too young to look for a job, so sometimes, on Saturdays, Gina and I would volunteer to help clean the school. The sisters in the convent taught us how to clean. I enjoyed that, but since I wasn't working at home or bringing any money in to Dad, I couldn't continue helping out for very long. I loved going to clean on Saturdays because Gina and I would talk to the nuns about God, heaven, and the saints and angels.

The convent had beautiful statues of Jesus with glass eyes. If you looked long enough, I think you could see heaven in the eyes. Sometimes, we would help dust the statues, but we had to do it very carefully.

"One day while we were doing our work, one of the nuns told us that there was something very serious going on at another church that had something to do with the Devil being real. Some priests were working at casting a devil out of someone. The nun told us to pray very hard. She wasn't allowed to say any more, but she did say that one of her cousins or her sister saw stuff going on at the priest's home and that it was very scary. She told us to be careful, because the Devil could come to us. We should keep Jesus in our hearts, she said. She told us to always cast Satan out when we felt he was bothering us.

"By the time I was in seventh grade, I was doing housecleaning and babysitting for the neighbors, and so were my sisters. Though we only made about ten or fifteen dollars a week, we had to give Dad at least half of what we made to help pay for the house. Sometimes, I would lie about how much I got from the jobs so that I could give a little to Mom. I felt sorry for her. She didn't get too much money to buy food for all of us.

"Another baby girl soon arrived. My parents named her Janet. There were seven of us kids. Dad complained about the money and the doctor, saying that the doctor had promised that they wouldn't have any more kids. He said we needed even more money than ever or else we'd all go to the poorhouse.

"Then, I remembered that Dad said that he should get money from the doctor for the last kid because they were guaranteed not to have any more. So, Dad called a lawyer. I remember that he got a check from the doctor. I think it was about a thousand dollars. This was something I wasn't supposed to know about, but I overheard them so many times on the phone with the lawyer, and I heard them talk about it over and over, plus I remember when they got the check. A man brought it over and made them sign some papers so I knew it was true.

"Dad said that as soon as we were able to get real jobs, we'd need to pay room and board every week. Around 1963, Helen was seventeen and Sadie was sixteen. They were both old enough to get out and find real jobs. They went out after school one day and each found a job at the same place, doing part-time work at Klaus Department Store. They worked after school and on Saturdays. Each had to pay thirty-five dollars for room and board weekly. The money went to my dad. As usual, nothing went to my mother.

"My dad made my brother, who was younger than me, move furniture. Jack was kept home from school many times to help Dad move furniture and boxes. Dad didn't pay Jack, so he was able to save more money by not calling a helper. Jack not only didn't get paid, he was also not allowed to keep any tips customers gave him. He had to give them to Dad. Dad said that if it wasn't for him, then Jack wouldn't have gotten the tip anyway. Therefore, Dad kept the money. Jack got a lot of tips because people said they liked him and that he did a good job. I wondered if they would have given him a tip if they knew his dad took it away from him.

"Dad had a lot of pictures of pin-up girls in his truck. He showed them to Jack and told him that it was okay to look. Jack said that lots of the women were naked and he was embarrassed but dad told him to be a man not a sissy.

"One day, Dad got mad at Jack and left him somewhere in the middle of the city. Jack had to go into a store and ask the owner to call my mom to come for him. He didn't know where he was. Jack was probably twelve or thirteen then.

"When Jack was fifteen, Dad made him take the truck out to make his deliveries. This was because Dad had a hangover. A hangover means that you drank too much beer the night before and were very sick in the morning and you would be throwing up. And my mom had to bring him a bucket to put by the bed. When Dad had a hangover, it was almost as bad as the fight the night before. He was loud and mean all day.

"Joe, Dad's boss from one of the department stores, called to ask where my dad was. Customers were expecting their deliveries. Dad was sleeping. My mom came to the bedroom to tell him that Joe called again and again. Dad yelled at my mom and told her, 'Tell him I don't care. I'm not working anymore. I'm fed up with work. You go to work and support these kids.'

"'Please, please, at least talk to him,' Mom would beg.

"'Have Jack do it,' Dad would bellow and laugh.

"'But Jack doesn't even have a driver's license. The truck is really big, and the items are too heavy for him to lift by himself,' my mom said, crying and nervous.

"Joe at the department store kept calling and warning my mom that if she didn't get my dad to do the jobs—as they were already promised—and that if Joe lost the sales, he would fire my dad. Mom was crying and really worried because Joe threatened never to call Dad again if he let him down. My mom knew we depended on Dad's pay for everything.

"Finally, my mom called one of Dad's helpers to help move the furniture with Jack. But that person didn't know how to drive, so Jack had to drive. Jack was scared, but he had no choice. We all walked over to the gas station with Jack. He pulled out the truck. He was a pretty cool kid. Actually, I was surprised that he could handle such a big truck. I was proud of him, but scared, too.

"All day long, my mom was scared and crying. My dad kept taunting her and telling her that if Jack and the helper got killed in an accident, it wasn't his fault. He said that he'd told my mom to tell Joe to get lost. He said that if anything bad happened to his truck, she'd pay. He said he would've let Joe fire him but she was willing to let her son get killed because she was so money-hungry. He laughed.

"Poor Jack. I can't believe he made it through the day. My dad took the money Jack got for the deliveries. He didn't pay Jack anything. Dad always picked on him and called him names. I felt so bad for Jack. I was mad at my dad for treating him that way. I wanted to tell him how mean I thought he was. But the next day came, and it was as if nothing happened. Nobody ever talked about the incident again. It would have caused trouble if someone reminded Dad of his hangover.

"One day, my dad and Jack had to deliver furniture to the projects, which was dangerous territory. Lots of robberies were reported in the area. My dad and Jack moved a sofa into an elevator and pressed the button to go upstairs. When they got out of the elevator, some guys with a gun came out of nowhere. At first, my dad held Jack in front of himself as a kind of shield and yelled 'Hey, I got a kid, I got a kid.' But when that didn't seem to make the would-be robbers go away, my dad pushed Jack away and took off, going back into the elevator. He told Jack to run. The elevator doors shut behind Dad, leaving Jack stuck on the top floor alone. My dad bolted for the truck, started it up, and pulled to the end of the block. He was safe in the truck, waiting for Jack. But he wasn't going to wait long if he saw anyone approaching.

"The robbers must have had a little heart. Since Jack was just a kid who didn't have any money, they let him go. Jack scrambled for the elevator and ran to the truck. Dad yelled at him to run, saying that he'd leave without him if he didn't hurry. Dad was already in first gear and had his foot on the brake. I think that Jack always felt a little bad because Dad hadn't waited for him, even at the building. Dad just shrugged it off and said he knew that Jack would be alright, because nobody would shoot a kid.

"When Jack was sixteen, he got a job at a gas station pumping gas and fixing cars. He made about a hundred and sixty dollars every two weeks. Dad took it all and told Jack that if he wanted any money, he could ask for it. I remember that one day Jack wanted to have twenty dollars to go out with his girlfriend. Dad started a fight and finally threw a ten at Jack. Jack never got any respect from my father. It hurt my feelings to know that my brother was treated so badly. I knew that Jack secretly cried a lot at night, because I could hear him. But I never let on that I heard because I think it would have made Jack feel worse. I wondered why God didn't help Jack; he was always being kicked around.

"I want to know more about you, too," I said.

"Okay. Stuff I want to tell you about me: The nuns had not only introduced me to Jesus, but they also taught me how to clean super good. By the time I was fourteen, I was really good at it. I worked cleaning houses for two neighbors. One day after cleaning one neighbor's house, I told my mom that the owner had grabbed me in a place where I didn't want to be grabbed. I told her he gave me five dollars and told me not to tell anyone. My mother laughed and took the money. I told her that I didn't want to clean for those neighbors anymore. She got real mad and told me that I was a troublemaker who was trying to start something in the neighborhood so that no one would like us. She said that I couldn't quit that job because I would have to give a good reason, and that reason would cause trouble for the neighbor and his wife. I hope you don't tell, because I don't want him to get into any trouble."

"Don't worry," I said. "I won't say anything."

"It was only a few months before I would be fifteen. I decided to start looking for another job. I knew that Mom would make me going back to that house. I also knew that if I didn't bring in any money, I'd be kicked out. So, when I turned fifteen, I got an application for a job at an A&P grocery store that had a help-wanted sign in the window. They wouldn't hire anyone under sixteen, so Dad told me to lie about my age and write down a phony Social Security number. He gave me a Social Security number to write down because I didn't have one of my own at that time. He told me that when I filled out my tax form, I should claim zero for dependents and then I would get more money. I didn't really understand that, but I claimed zero dependents. I did what he told me and got the job. I worked after school and on Saturdays. My take-home pay was about seventy dollars a week. Dad cashed my checks and took out thirty-five dollars a week for room and board.

"At the end of the year, I got a tax form. Dad said he'd take care of it for me. He took care of the tax forms for Helen and Sadie, too. When I got a refund check, he made me sign it on the back. Sometimes, I didn't know how much it was. He always kept it. He told me that the amount was what it cost to figure out the forms. I didn't quite understand all that, but I thought that some of that money belonged to me. However, I didn't say anything! I didn't want to start any trouble.

"I wanted to go to art school when I was done with high school. I loved painting and sculpting with clay. But my dad said that after high school, I'd be eighteen and would have to move out. He said that if I intended to live at home, I had to get a job and pay full-time room and board, about a hundred dollars a week. That would leave no time or money for school.

"Helen, Sadie, and I had learned typing in school. We had to type bills for my dad's business. In our school typing class, we were encouraged to do some typing at home for extra credit. But we couldn't get any extra credit for typing his bills because we had to set the tabs in such a way that made it impossible to practice what we learned in school.

We asked Dad to let us change the tabs or if he would, at least, change the place where he put the notes. He laughed at us and refused. It was a terribly tedious job. It was like typing backward. Needless to say, we didn't get any money from dad for doing his bills.

"Our homework had to wait if he wanted his bills typed. He said that his bills were more important than our schoolwork. We'd never know when he'd want a bill typed. If we'd planned to go out or do something and he said that he needed a bill done, then we would have to change our plans.

"We still got our underpants pulled down for spankings. He would bend us over the table to spank us with the pitta or belt, but there were two fewer straps on the pitta. One of us, I'm not telling who, broke off two of the straps and threw them away. As teenagers, getting our pants pulled down was really embarrassing: sometimes it was that time of the month. But there was no age limit for one of Dad's beatings. We also had other punishments: kneeling on blocks, eating mashed potatoes mixed with long pieces of hair, washing the dishes in ice-cold water, cleaning the floor with a toothbrush, things like that. Dad always said, 'I figure it this way. I made youse, so I can do whatever I want with youse.'

There were still big fights when dad started his drinking. They still lasted all night long and they were still pretty violent. One time he cracked my mom's wrist. I think it was broken.

"We went to a Catholic school. Our tuition was always delinquent. Sometimes, it was still unpaid at the end of the year. Helen, my oldest sister, worked her way through one year by washing windows for twenty-five cents each. It was very hard for her. She still had to keep her job at the department store so she could pay room and board. She hardly had time to even wash her hair!

"I still prayed a lot of rosaries and went to church pretty regularly. I even joined the Third Order of St. Francis. That was like a real dedication to the Lord. You had to say a lot of prayers every day. It was kind of like pre-training to see if you wanted to become a nun. But I couldn't go to all the meetings after school. Also, I didn't have time to say all the prayers because I had to work. So, I dropped out of the Third Order.

"I did so well at my job at the grocery store that they wanted me to go to their bookkeeping school so I could learn how to do payroll and stuff after graduation. But it was for two weeks of training with no pay. Dad said I'd still have to pay thirty-five dollars a week for room and board or else he'd kick me out. I didn't have enough money for that. I had to decline the bookkeeping offer because I had no place to go and was still in school. Dad told me that if I wanted to go to any school and not bring in any money, then I should go find someplace else to live.

"One day, Dad came to pick me up after work. He told the assistant manager that he heard that I was pretty good at my job. Ed agreed and told him that I was a really hard worker. Dad told Ed that he should stick a broom up my butt so I could sweep the floors while I was walking up the aisles and stocking shelves. My face turned completely red when my dad said that, but I pretended not to hear. My dad and Ed both laughed outrageously. I was very humiliated.

"After that, lots of times, Ed would laugh and tell me that he had a broom and that I should bend over. I always pretended not to hear. Still, that became a regular joke when other employees were around. I didn't look forward to going to work anymore. I started to look at other grocery stores that might need help.

"I started a little bank account, but Mom and Dad found out. Dad said that if I was rich enough to afford a bank account, then I should pay more money. He raised my room and board to fifty dollars per week. That left me with twenty or twenty-five dollars. I had no money for anything except a few records here and there. I was always very nervous. It always seemed that I couldn't get enough money to make Mom or Dad happy. Mom was always asking to 'borrow a few dollars.' Finally, I just closed the bank account. It was impossible to save any money at that time.

"In '63, I got more hours at work and was able to save a bit, all in silver dimes. Then, around '65, I started saving Kennedy silver half-dollars. I saved them in a five-gallon water jar I'd found in the alley and hidden in my closet.

"One time, I found Dad in the closet taking coins out of the bottle. He said that he was trading the silver money for other coins because the silver ones worked better in the pay phones. He said that the value was the same. But after a while, it seemed to me that I had a lot fewer coins in there than I thought I should have had. I suppose I was selfish for trying to save money for myself when Mom and Dad needed it so much.

"Mom had to keep us home from school many times to help her clean house and do the ironing that she took in from neighbors in order to make a few dollars. But she couldn't let Dad know, because he would have taken the money, saying that the ironing was costing extra for electricity. So, as soon as Mom finished her ironing, we'd have to run it over to the neighbors before Dad could see.

"Most weeks, Mom had to beg Dad for food money. Sometimes, he'd give her the money on time. Other times, he made her wait. Many times, he'd imitate her begging and make fun of her. One time, I remember he tore up all the dollars he gave her for food money, throwing the pieces at her. He also removed the 'bug wire' from the car so she couldn't use it. The bug wire was a rubber-coated wire that went from the distributor cap to the ignition coil to make the car start. The car wouldn't start without the bug wire. Later, Jack and I learned where our dad hid it. Jack showed me a lot about cars. We'd find the bug wire and put it in the car so Mom could use the car. We would chalk the street and leave a chair in place so she could park the car exactly where Dad had left it. But after a while, he found out what we were doing, since he marked the mileage on the car. After that, he took the bug wire with him when he went out. Anyway, back to the torn dollars. We all helped to tape the pieces together and then walked to the store, but the store wouldn't take the taped-up dollars. We had to walk a long way to the bank to trade them in. We had to wait a long time at the bank. I guess they had to make sure that all the dollars fit together properly.

"The nightly fights continued in the new house. Dad was louder and began using more filthy language. He already had so many bad words, but each time he added new ones! Some of the things I still can't figure out. Like, he said we all had paper ... can I say it?"

"Sure. Whatever it is, it's between us."

"Okay, he said we all had paper butts. But I don't know what that means, so maybe it's not so bad, anyway. He said over and over that Mom and us girls were all nothing but pieces of stink. You'd think he would have stopped that by now. When Dad thought we were ignoring him, he'd pick one of us, usually Jack, and pull him out of bed to make him sit down at the table and listen.

"Jack was told that when he got older, he should kick his mother and his sisters because, 'All women are all like boats. They're all the same. They're all no good.' Dad told Jack that he couldn't wait till my mother was dead so he could spit on her grave. He said, 'I wouldn't give her the sweat from under my left arm.'

"I never did get the boat reference, but I felt bad thinking about my mother being in a grave. And I couldn't understand why my dad would think that it was something my mother wanted, you know, the sweat under his left arm. I mean, who would want that, anyway? So, what should she care if he didn't give it to her? Yuck!

"My mom told Dad to be quiet because he'd wake the neighbors. The neighbors' bedroom was right next to where Dad was yelling. It was summer, so all the windows were open. Mom told him that George, our next door neighbor who was Gina's dad, had to get up at 5:00 a.m. to go to work. She didn't want the neighbors to know that she and my dad were fighting. Then, just for spite, my dad went to the window, opened it really wide, and yelled, 'Hey, Georgie, you worthless sack of garbage, you wanna fight me? Come on out, you stupid jerk, sissy boy!' to Gina's dad. It was embarrassing. Gina was in the same grade as me. We usually walked to school together. One time I asked her how it was when her mom and dad fought, if she was scared. But she told me that they didn't fight, so we never talked about it again.

"Then, my parents' fight escalated and my mom said those words that she had said a long time ago about what my dad had done to 'his own daughter'. But this time it was *daughters,* you know, plural.

"And then, like a flash, I remembered something. It was from when I was about twelve or thirteen years old. One time early in the morning while I was sleeping, I felt someone's hands on me, all over me, where they shouldn't be. I got up and screamed real loud. The person left my room and went downstairs. My mom must have been at the store because when I came downstairs she wasn't there. When she got home, I told my mom what had happened, and she said that I must have been dreaming. I think she knew but pretended not to know. She probably didn't want to say anything or cause any trouble. I don't think this was the only time this kind of thing happened, but I don't want to remember any more times.

"Years later, I realized who it was. I figured out that I was supposed to pretend I was asleep when it happened. But we kids were told not to say anything, lest we would cause a big fight. So, I kept quiet about it.

"But my dad didn't bother me much after that. At least, I don't remember that he did. But I did notice that after that, he took an unusual interest in Martha, asking her to sit and watch television with him and wanting to teach her to drive. But she didn't want to go. Also, Mom said if Dad took Martha for driving lessons, then Jack and I had to go with. Dad did not want us to go with. One time we poked our heads in the front seat and saw, well his hands weren't on the steering wheel. Martha was kind of crying and Dad got real mad at us.

"I guess I caused the big fight that day. You see all the fights I caused? You see how bad I was? It's my fault Justin's gone! It is, isn't it? God took him because I was bad—because you were bad and deserve to be punished!"

The little girl was shouting. Then, she started crying. I was hoping to reflect on what she said, about me being bad, but before I could, she turned from me and tried to run away. I reached for her and turned her body around to face me.

"Don't hit me! Don't hit me!" she said. She rolled on the ground and covered her head.

"I won't hit you. I won't hit you! No, no, you weren't bad, no, not at all! It's not your fault! God doesn't work that way," I said, even though I couldn't be sure that what I was saying was true.

The girl calmed down after a few minutes. She said, "Yeah … maybe. Well, I wasn't the only bad one. I wasn't the only one who caused trouble. My sister Martha caused trouble one time, I remember now. She caused a lot of trouble! She was seventeen. She had only a part-time job—not enough hours to pay her own way, Dad said. But she got really sick. Her own fault, dad said. The doctor said she needed an operation. Some kind of tumor broke and was bleeding inside her. She didn't have any insurance. My dad was mad that she didn't have a full-time job with insurance. He said she'd be eighteen in a few months and that she wouldn't be his responsibility then.

"He argued with my mom. He said he only had insurance for himself, which he paid for with his own hard-earned money. He said he wasn't going to be paying for anyone else's health problems. He refused to pay for the operation. But Martha needed it right away. Dad said that was tough luck. 'Let her go to County Hospital,' he said. 'She should have thought about this before and bought some insurance.' Mom didn't have any money, so she couldn't help out. Dad told Martha to go to the state and ask for assistance or take out a loan or wait till she was eighteen, get some insurance and pay for her own operation. He said she wasn't his problem. 'I paid enough for these kids, and I'm not paying anymore.'

"Martha was just seventeen. No bank would give her a loan. So, my mom talked to the hospital and arranged a loan with Harris Bank so Martha could get her operation. Martha was too young to sign, so my mom signed with her. Martha had to make payments over several years until she finally paid for her own operation.

"When Jack had a regular job and didn't work with my dad anymore, my littlest brother, Erik, had to take his place. By the time Erik was in high school, he couldn't join in any after-school activities. Dad was usually there at the end of the school day to pick him up and make him help out with deliveries. Erik didn't get paid but was told that he would be kicked out of the house if he didn't pay his way by working for Dad.

"When Erik was almost finished with high school, he took a civil service test. He wanted to be a postal worker. Erik passed the test and was called in for an interview after school. Dad drove him to the interview but warned him to tell the people that he wouldn't be ready to start until his dad gave him the okay. He told him if he didn't, then he'd come home one day and all his stuff would be on the lawn because he wouldn't be allowed to live in the house. He'd have to find his own place right away.

"Erik did what Dad told him to do, but the post office told him that they needed him right away. If he couldn't start right away, then they would get someone else. So, Erik lost out on that opportunity and kept working for my dad.

"Dad was all about money. As my brother Erik got older, he finally insisted that Dad pay him to help with the deliveries. So, for working six days a week, Erik made two hundred dollars. Although Dad paid Erik cash, he subtracted money for room and board and the lunches he bought Erik. They would stop at hot dog places. Dad would make up a list of how much money he spent on Erik's food and where and when they ate.

"I remember that around that time, my dad started buying stocks. He didn't tell my mother he was buying stocks because he didn't want her to know how much money he had. They had an argument one day, and my mother found he was really upset because he'd lost five thousand dollars on some stocks.

"Dad never took my mother on any vacations. My mother always wanted to go to Hawaii or Disneyland. He told her they didn't have enough money, but she knew by then that he did have the money. She didn't know how much, but she knew it was enough for a vacation. She felt really bad. He always told her they had no money to go out to eat, order a pizza, see a movie, or go on any vacations—and no money to pay for my sister's operation. But now my mom knew that our dad was buying stocks and making investments without her knowing and without her name being on anything. She was mad at him because he wouldn't pay for my sister's operation yet was willing to lose five thousand dollars on stock he didn't know anything about.

"The fights got so bad about Martha's operation that, one time, my father dumped over the entire refrigerator with all the food in it. Mom just cleaned things up the next day. Nothing ever changed. Life went on as before.

"Although Helen, Sadie, and I had part-time jobs, since we were so good at babysitting, we got a referral to sit for a little girl who had severe Down's syndrome. Her mom paid more than the regular wage for babysitting. My sisters and I were able to fit in the time to sit even though we had jobs. The girl's parents, Glen and Rose, didn't want to put her in an institution because they felt she could get better care at home. She was seven and a really pretty girl. Her parents padded a room for her to play in. It was hard to watch her as she got bigger, because we couldn't hold her down to change her and she got too heavy to pick up. But we did a good job of watching Claudia until she got into biting us.

"Claudia's parents were really nice. They were both professors. Her father was also a professional magician. The parents were pretty sophisticated. Mom and Dad met them and invited them over to our house. At some point in the evening, they were talking and laughing. The man put his arm around my mom just as a hugging gesture. I saw it. I thought it was a nice thing to do. My dad grabbed Glen by the collar and started punching him. He accused him of trying to do things with my mom, the same things he said the milkman and the other guys had done. My dad pushed Glen through a glass door. There was blood all over.

"My mom was horrified. She tried to pull Dad off Glen, but Dad started pushing her. I don't remember the rest, because we kids were told to get upstairs. Each of us was saying, 'Mom, please don't say anything.' We knew that if she or one of us said the wrong thing, then there'd be more trouble.

"The police came over, but nobody went to jail or anything. Come to think of it, the police came over several times during those days. But nothing ever happened as a result. Mom always told the police that she didn't want to sign the complaint hat would put my dad in jail."

"Didn't you have any friends? Did you ever go out on any dates?" I asked.

"I don't think anyone really liked me. Sometimes, I'd get asked out. When the boy didn't show up, everyone laughed at me. That hurt my feelings more than the boy's not showing up. So, if anyone ever did invite me on a date, and hardly anyone ever did, I usually said, 'No, thanks.'"

The little girl turned her head to one side and seemed to be listening to something.

"What is it? What's wrong?" I asked.

"Quickly, quickly, do you forgive me? Do you? There! Do you hear it? The voices, they are real. You have to go." She pointed deeper into the swamp. "There, there is where you'll find your answers. I can't say anymore. I can't!"

"But I didn't ask the questions I wanted to. I don't have my answers, the things I need to know," I said.

"You must go now. If you do, then maybe, maybe I'll see you again on your way out, if you learn to forgive—me, forgive yourself."

"There's nothing to forgive. What are you talking about? Forgive by myself? I don't understand. Also, I can't leave you here. The monsters, they—"

"He'll watch over me," the girl said, holding up her Jesus statue. "But I hope you'll come back. Please come back for me!"

"I don't want to go. Where am I supposed to go? I don't even know this place."

She pointed the way, and then a thick fog engulfed us. I felt something swoop down over my head. Then, something big with coarse fur scurried across my feet. I jumped away. When I looked back, I didn't see the little girl. I was farther into the swamp than I had thought. Dark was all around. I moved slowly.

BSA Baby, 1967

In the distance, I heard a loud motor rumbling and a voice singing and swearing obscenities. It was an angry voice. The motor and the voice were a very threatening combination. The cacophony of sound was getting nearer. I was filled with dread. I began walking slowly in the direction the little girl had pointed, but I was scared because that was the direction from which the noise was coming.

O Jesus, I prayed, *please be with me. Don't leave me here alone.*

I saw a single dim light coming toward me. I hid behind an old tree with gnarly roots. I was sure that whoever was behind the rumbling sound wouldn't find me there. Barely uttering a breath, I clung to the tree.

As the light got closer, I could see that it was on a kind of motorcycle. It had a green glow with fire spewing out the sides. I was surprised by how fast it could go through the tangles in the swamp, riding through trees and over water filled with creatures that were coming alive, reaching up, and biting at the air. But the motorcycle ran smooth and fast. It came menacingly close. It slowly circled the tree I was hiding behind. I tried to break and run.

"I see you tryin' ta hide. Stop where you are. You can't run from me."

I stopped. My heart was pounding. I was alone, too far in to turn back. I had come for answers, just answers. I hadn't found any, so I should have just turned back and left. I reached for the handle in my pocket to make sure the knife was still there. *This is it,* I thought, *time to make use of my knife, time to say good-bye.* I wondered how I had gotten into this mess. But it was too late. Suddenly, the bike was in front of me, pinning me against the tree. I couldn't get my hand out of my pocket, I couldn't even move. Even if I did, where would I run?

"Sit down!" the loud voice ordered. "I know why you're here. You and me, we got lots to talk about," a female said in an accusatory tone.

"I'm not here for you. What do you want?" I asked.

"It's not what I want, it's what *you* want. And you're gonna get it. What you do with it is up to you."

The rider pulled off her helmet and shook out her long brown hair. She was a young woman. At first glance, I thought she was pretty, but upon closer inspection, I saw that her hair was tangled and dirty. There was a small patch of skin on her head. It looked as though the hair there had been torn out. The young woman's face was scarred. Her body had lots of bites wherever her skin was showing. Some were old and some were fresh. One of her teeth was missing or broken. Her nails, what there was of them, were coated with black grease and looked pretty chewed up. She smelled old and dirty.

"You were with the little girl. I knew she'd send you here. In a way, I was hoping she would … but I really didn't want to be found."

"I wasn't looking to find you. I don't even know who you are. Wait, you know the girl?" I asked.

"Yeah, the little girl, yeah, I know her. Well, I did for a while."

"Who is she? I want to get back to her. I have to help her. Who are you?"

"It don't matter right now. You and me, we gotta lot in common. Now, you wanna sit down and listen?"

"No, no, I don't. I don't care what you have to say. Who are you, anyway?"

"Tra-la-la." In a strange-sounding and most annoying voice, she sang, actually sang: "That's for me to know and for you to find out."

"Why should I care? What do you know that could help me?" I asked.

"You'd be surprised at what I know. What did you come here for, anyway?"

"I'm here to find out if there is a God and why He took my boy. I don't want to talk to you. You wouldn't have anything to say that I want to hear. Forget about the questions. Even if there is a God, you wouldn't know anything about Him. And He wouldn't want anything to do with you. And my boy, he's too good to talk to you about. I want to get out of here now."

"Well, you're right about one thing, He wouldn't have anything to do with me. But you, Ms. Righteous, you came out here to find out if there is a God? What are ya doin' here? Why ain't you in church?"

"I just … I don't know how I got here, but I want to—"

"Shut up! Here's the rules, my rules: You shut up. I talk. You listen. Sit yourself down, 'cause if you don't listen to me now, you'll never get out of here. I won't let you."

The young woman was coarse and rude. I didn't want to be there. "There's some mix-up. Something's wrong! All I care about is my son, my beautiful son," I sobbed. "So, go ahead, kill me, if that's what you're here to do! I don't care about you! I don't care about you, you … pig! You filthy piece of st—" I stopped when I realized what I had almost said.

"Of stink? Yeah, that's about right, huh, from you. Well, let me tell ya something. You'll care about me, about what I say. I can guarantee you will."

She was way stronger than I. She pushed me to the ground and went over to one of the saddlebags on her bike. She pulled out a bottle of wine. "Wanna slug?"

"No. I don't drink."

"Oh yeah, oh, really?" She laughed. "Well, I do. Let's start by talking about me. Okay with you?"

I shook my head and held my hand over my face.

"Well, who cares what you think? I got da floor, as they say. I was third in a family of seven. By the time I was eighteen, it was obvious that everyone was in a mad competition to get ol' Dad's attention. Everyone wanted him to like them best or, at least, to like them. Mom, well, maybe that mattered, but not that much. Guess everyone just got the idea she nat'urly cared about 'em."

"I don't want to know about you or your family! I don't care."

"You will, I tell ya, you will."

I stared at her.

"What you lookin' at? Dis little bald spot on my head, I see."

"No, I'm sorry. It's none of my business," I said. I was starting to feel like Alice in Wonderland. This is all so crazy. I'm actually talking to, what, a monster.

"Yeah, it is. It is. It is your business." The young woman looked off sadly into the distance, paused, and began talking again. "Dad, he liked to sit on da sofa and pull our hair. Yeah, dat's right, pull our hair. All of us girls had longer hair. Sadie and Martha got the worst of it. Me and Helen, well, we had our hair kinda short. Anyway, he'd wind his fingers around our hair and pull. Sometimes, he'd pull so hard that we'd let out a squeal. Then, he'd get mad and push us away and say we were looking to start trouble. See, that's what this patch up here is from." She pointed to a small balding spot on her head. "Ain't my fault, didn't do it myself. He pulled it out, and it never grew back. Never grew back."

She grew quiet and shook her head in disbelief. "Sometimes, I think he just liked to hurt us. Actually, it's true. He did like to hurt us. Anyway, don't make no difference now. None of us liked it, but we had to let him do it or else we'd cause trouble and he'd get mad—and that was worse than getting your hair pulled out."

She looked off in the distance as if seeing the past on a movie screen. She sighed and settled in a little. Her tough façade seemed to fade as she returned to speaking. "My two older sisters, Helen and Sadie, had moved out and gotten married a couple of years or so before I got out.

"Sadie, my second-oldest sister, was the first out the door. She got married to a guy who was studying to be a pilot. Dad always laughed at Bill, but not to his face. He'd tell us that Bill was going to learn to take a mound of dirt and pile it here and then pile it there. That's the only kind of 'pile-it' he would ever be. Dad said that Bill was a lazy bum who just wanted to go to school to waste time. And Dad was sure that no one who was smart enough to be a pilot would marry any of his daughters.

"Helen got out about a year later. She married a childhood sweetheart. So, both Helen and Sadie made the deadline: out at eighteen, or very close to it!

"Now, it was my turn. My mom and dad were really anxious to get me to move out. They told me I should start looking for someone to marry. Can you believe that? The deal was that you got married by eighteen or else you got kicked out. I'd go to church and pray that I'd find someone, but I was afraid I wouldn't. I thought I was just plain too ugly. I was, you know. Still am, I guess. I scrapped the idea of being a nun because your parents would have to pay a dowry to the church. No way was that ever going to happen.

"Mom kept urging me to go out and meet someone anywhere. She even asked me if there was a chance that I didn't like boys. She was worried that maybe I was, ya know, a queer. Can you imagine that, just 'cause I didn't have boys calling me? Then again, girls weren't calling me, either. So, I don't know why she said that.

"I didn't have any friends, not even one or two. I wasn't what you would call popular. Of the A, B, and C groups, I was probably in the D-minus. That's just how it was. I told my mom that I didn't want to go out with just anyone. I wanted to meet a special someone. She laughed and told me that I should get real. I would never meet someone like that. She said that was a fairy tale. She said that some girls had a choice because they were real pretty and popular. But I wouldn't get a choice unless I was at least popular, which I wasn't. She said if I was lucky enough to get anyone to ask me I better say yes before he changed his mind because time was wasting. But my prospects looked dim since I wasn't going out with anyone.

"When I was almost out of high school, I met this boy, Jimmy. I thought he was kind of creepy, as did the other girls. He was what we called a 'fast' boy. He kept coming over the house, asking me to go out. But I told my mom that if he came over, she should tell him I wasn't home because he'd always be trying to, well, you know, put his hands all over me. Mom said that meant he liked me. I could see a glimmer of hope in her eyes, thinking that someone would actually want to put his hands on me and that he might be my future husband. Guess I should have been flattered. But I thought that Jimmy was a creep.

"My mom said I should go out with him because his feelings might be hurt if I refused. I told her I didn't like him. I told her that none of the other girls liked him, either. I reminded her how he was always grabbing me. She told me I should let him do what he wanted, at least a little, because to refuse him would hurt his feelings. He'd think that nobody liked him. I don't know what she meant by 'at least a little,' but even a little was too much for me. Yuck!"

She took a slug from the bottle, gargled, and spit out the wine. She looked at me. "Yeah, I'm a slob. So what? Anyway, Ma said, 'You gotta go out with this guy,' so I went out with him a few times, but I didn't like it. He might not have gotten his feelings hurt the first few times I went out with him, but, eventually, I had to hurt his feelings. I dumped him. Mom was always making me go out with guys that no one else liked just so their feelings wouldn't be hurt. I could hardly stand it! Short guys, fat guys, pimply guys, really dumb guys and some very strange guys … all losers. But I guess I was a loser, too, at least in her eyes."

The young woman reached into her pocket for cigarettes and then offered me one. "No, no, thanks," I said. She lit the cigarette. It looked like a cigarette but smelled like a dead skunk. I guess she didn't notice, because she just puffed away. She seemed to hold the smoke in for a long time before she started coughing. It didn't look like the cigarette agreed with her, but I wasn't going to comment on that.

"Mom was really getting worried. No one, I mean no one, not even any of the losers, was calling me. So, she decided to give me tips on how to get a guy. She was worried that nobody liked me, so she tried to help enhance my 'attractivity.' Ha! Impossible! First of all, she told me to stop talking about cars. Then, Mom told me that maybe boys didn't like me because I was trying to be smart. She said I should act stupid, really stupid. Now, that wasn't going to be too much of a stretch for me!

"She told me that even if I knew the correct answer to a question, I should give a wrong answer, because that would make the boys feel better when they gave the right answer. She said that girls should always act dumb. She said that boys would like me better if they thought they were smarter than me. 'No boy ever wants to go out with a smart girl,' she said. I usually tried to do what I was told. I was convinced that everyone else knew what to say and do. Sometimes, it was hard not to go my own way, but then, in my heart, I didn't really believe I knew the right thing to say or do. So, I tried it out one day. What a bust! So, listen to this …"

"Will this take long? I have questions. I'm not here to listen to all your garbage, all your vulgarity!" I said.

"What did I tell you when you got here? The rules, what were the rules?" She grabbed me by the collar and stuck her dirty face in mine. She smelled like old wine and skunky smoke. It wasn't a pleasant smell. "Yeah, I'm vulgar. I'm loud. But I ain't shuttin' up no more, not me. So what? I talk; you shut up and listen!"

"Okay! Okay!" I pulled away from her. It was a relief to breathe fresher air.

"At that time, I belonged to a choir at church. Can ya believe it, a choir?"

"No, I can't."

"Ah, who cares what you think, anyway? I oughta smack you one. Anyway, the guy who led the choir was going to have a birthday, and all of us girls knew he was turning thirty. We made little cards and were going to give them to him at practice.

"I told my mom, and she said that I should pretend not to know his age and to ask him if he was going to be twenty. I told her I knew he was going to be thirty. She said that this would be a great time to practice what she told me. I should act dumb because he'd like it if he thought the girls thought he was just twenty. She said that men like to think they look younger than they are. 'Then when he tells you he's going to be thirty, smile and say, "Oh, I didn't know! You look so young, just like a teenager!"' she said.

"I really didn't want to do it, but she was very firm about this and said that it would make him feel very pleased to know he looked so young. He would appreciate it. She said it would be good practice in getting boys to like me.

"Well, I have to admit, I wanted to please people, so I said it to him. I don't know why I listened to her. I said it in front of all the other girls. After I did, he looked at me in amazement and said so seriously, 'Jane, you know I'm going to be thirty. I told everyone in class. Why would you say this to me?' The girls, who had been quiet at first, started laughing. I just said, 'I don't know. You look so young, like a teenager.' As the words came out of my mouth, I felt like I was in third grade on Halloween, wearing that stupid costume to school. I smiled with this stupid smile, like a big jerk. The choir director just shook his head in disgust and walked away. Then, he and the rest of the choir began calling me Zanie Janie. Don't look at me that way! I was just following orders, as they say."

The young woman took another slug from the bottle and then offered it to me. I shook my head. "Suit yourself," she said. She swallowed gulp after gulp. "Then, I got more interested in cars and tried to get a job at a body shop or gas station. My brother and me, we liked to work on cars. He taught me stuff, so I knew somethin' about how to fix them. But I guess that didn't matter. They didn't hire girls at that time. The guys just laughed at me. But my interest in cars led me to meet a mechanic. His name was John. He was just newly divorced, and he actually liked me. We dated and then he proposed to me. Can you believe it? I actually hooked someone when I wasn't even trying. How do you like that? I didn't really want to marry a divorced man who was eight years older than me, but Mom said I was real lucky I'd finally found someone. She said I'd never find anyone again and that my time was running out. I was already eighteen. If I didn't grab up my only chance of getting a man to marry me, then Dad was going to kick me out. My dad liked John a lot because he'd fix Dad's car for free. So, I said yes. John got me an engagement ring.

"Things were alright for a while. We dated, went to car races, stuff like that. He showed me how to speed-shift and drag race. Then, I began to see that he had a mean streak in him. At first, it was little things, like saying something rude to a waitress, telling dirty jokes in front of his friends to embarrass me, or driving a little too aggressively on the street and cutting other cars off. At first, I tried to ignore it.

"Sometimes when we went out, he'd leave his dog in the house alone. Then, he'd get really mad if the dog messed up. Pretty often, he'd beat that dog like crazy. He'd actually lift him up and throw him down the stairs. I felt sorry for the dog. It was a purebred German shepherd. I was surprised it didn't bite him. But the dog was really a friendly dog in spite of all the beatings. And honestly, up to that point, I'd seen my dad do a lot of mean things, so I thought that maybe this was pretty normal. I didn't say anything. I didn't want to start any trouble.

"But one day, we were at a McDonald's. We were sitting in John's car when I saw a customer standing at the counter. When the manager behind the counter turned around, the customer kind of set herself down on the floor in a sprawling posture and started screaming, 'I fell. I fell on this dirty floor. I'm going to sue you.' Well, I saw what really happened. I told John that I saw what happened and that I knew she did not really fall. She was lying. John told me to stay in the car and shut up. He said it was none of my business. I said I couldn't, because that wouldn't be the right thing to do. He said, 'I told you once already to stay in the car.' I said that it would only take a minute and I'd be right back. So, I got out of the car and gave the manager my name and phone number. He wrote down what I said. When I got back in the car, John punched me in the face. He shouted, 'I told you to stay in the car!'

My nose was bleeding. Any feelings I had for John left that second. I got out of the car and walked home. When I got home, my mom asked me where I was, because John had been calling all evening. I told her what had happened, that he had hit me. She laughed and said, 'Maybe you deserved it.' Well, here's to that! I guess he knew you were bad, too. I wonder if John has a pitta at home. Ha! Or maybe Dad could give him one for a wedding present. Yeah, just what I always wanted, a pitta of my own!"

She held up the bottle as if to give a toast and then took a swig. She belched offensively. I said nothing. I pretended I hadn't heard, didn't want to cause trouble.

"I told her I was giving his ring back. Dad and Mom were really mad at me and said that I'd better start looking for somewhere to live. I didn't care.

"Though John kept coming around, I told him it was over. I couldn't stand him! You know, it's really icky to have someone kiss you when all of a sudden you can't stand him."

I nodded and agreed. I understood what she was saying. I was getting lost in this woman's stories even though I didn't want to. I didn't know how they would give me any insight into what I needed to know. All I knew was that it was best to keep my mouth shut and listen. Otherwise, I might never get out of there.

"A couple of days later, there was another big fight at home. Dad was threatening Mom, but this time I yelled back at him to leave her alone. He came at me with a knife. Mom made me hide in the bedroom. She and Martha were pulling the door closed while my dad was trying to pull it open. So, my mom made me sneak out through the bedroom window. Fortunately, this was one of the bedrooms on the first floor, so I didn't have far to drop. Mom told me not to come back that night. She said I should have kept my mouth shut. She said I was nothing but a troublemaker. So, I drove around in my old Ford for a while till I got tired. Then, I parked it and went to sleep.

"By this time, I wasn't working at the neighborhood A&P anymore. I had found a job working as a food checker at a market about ten miles from home in a little suburb. There was a plumbing company right next door to the grocery market. Every day after work, as I was heading to my car, I'd see this really cute plumber. He had a BSA motorcycle, and he looked really good. I had a thing for bikes, anyway, and, well, up close, this guy looked really hot, if you know what I mean. I don't know how, but suddenly I knew he was the man I'd been waiting for. I knew he was the one. I don't know how, but I just knew. Every day, I saw him. Every day, I hoped he'd at least say hi or whistle or something. But he didn't. It was like he never even saw me. I wasn't going to wait for him to notice me, 'cause it looked like that would never happen. I wasn't a 'noticeable' person.

"I decided to introduce myself. I didn't want this one to get away. I knew that if I didn't make some attempt to meet him, I would always be sorry. I figured if he brushed me off I could take it. I was used to being brushed off anyway. And there was always that chance that he might not brush me off. He introduced himself as Charlie. I came right to the point and asked him for a ride on his bike. He told me that I was wearing a dress and should bring some long pants to wear. If I did, then he would take me for a ride. Can you believe this guy, telling a girl that he can't take her out unless she gets some pants on? I thought it should be just the opposite! But this guy was worth the effort, so I threw a pair of pants into my car and waited weeks for him to make good on his promise. One day, he finally came into the store when I was at the register and asked me if I brought my pants. I told him I did. He said he had time to take me for a bike ride after work. Five o'clock came around, and I dashed to the car to get my pants on. I was ready for that ride. I pretended that I'd been on bikes before so I would sound cool, but, actually, this was my first ride on one. We rode and talked, talked a lot. I got a little cold, so he took off his sweatshirt and let me wear it. It smelled good. Then, he just had his T-shirt on. I knew he was cold, but he gave up his shirt for me. I liked that. This guy, Charlie, he had a good, clean heart. He seemed a little elusive about dating me, but I could tell that he liked me at least a little. Still, he was moving pretty slow.

"So, I was still wondering if I could ever get a guy so cool to really like me, I mean, big-time liking. Know what I mean? I talked about him to Sue, one of the other checkers who worked with me. She said she'd try to accidently meet him and casually see what he thought of me. But before I knew it, she was offering to give him back massages and cook up a dinner for him. This I did not want. So, I had to get myself out there to talk more to Charlie, since Sue was actually trying to get him to take her out. Wow, I couldn't trust Sue, that's for sure.

"Anyway, to continue, my mom still wanted me to go back with the mechanic because he was a sure thing. Plus, John kept calling and coming over to the house. But I didn't want to go back with him. Charlie would stop at the store from time to time and take me for more bike rides. I kept those pants readily available in the car. I can't say that we ever really went on a date. We would just meet after work and get something to eat and then go for a bike ride. When I told my mom that Charlie wanted to marry me, she didn't believe me. She said it was impossible that two guys actually wanted to marry me. She called me a liar and told me that I was just trying to buy time so I wouldn't get kicked out. Anyway, she said that anyone who rides a motorcycle is a hood and probably a killer.

"Ultimately, she found that I was not lying. And my dad was happy that Charlie was a plumber. He figured he could get work done around the house for free.

"Charlie and I were going to have just a small wedding. Neither of us knew a lot of people, and we didn't have a lot of money. But Mom wanted me to have a big wedding with all the family, so we let her make all the plans. She invited about a hundred and twenty-five people. We didn't even know them all, but that was okay. We were really in love and wanted to be together. For the first time, I felt I was actually in charge of my own life.

"We had a church wedding. My dad walked me up the aisle. When he handed me off to Charlie, he shook Charlie's hand, rolled his eyes, and said very loudly, 'Thank you, oh, thank you.' That wasn't the way it had been rehearsed. I didn't think that was very funny, but I wasn't going to make a big thing about it. *Don't say anything. Don't start any trouble.*

"I paid for my dress, and Charlie paid for flowers and the band and extras. We didn't have the money for the hall or the food for the big wedding my mom wanted, so my dad said he would put up the money and we could pay it back with whatever monetary gifts we got. Traditionally, in our family, everyone gave money, not gifts.

"It was a funny thing, but all the money we got as gifts, about thirty-seven hundred dollars, was, according to my dad, the exact cost of the wedding.

"Later, I figured it out. The hall offered open bar and family-style food for less than twelve bucks a person. We had about a hundred and twenty-five guests. That didn't equal thirty-seven hundred dollars. He shouldn't have kept all our money. But I didn't want to say anything, didn't want to make any trouble.

"After the wedding, when it was time for me to move out, Dad told me that I wasn't allowed to take anything but my clothes. Dad said that the toys, books, comic books, transistor radio, records, anything I'd bought, the coins I'd saved, the encyclopedias I'd won, all my art pictures, and anything else I'd gotten while I was 'under his roof' was his. He also made Charlie pay him two hundred dollars, the balance due on an old car he had sold me a few years before. I hadn't paid my dad the balance because the car threw a rod shortly after he sold it to me and I had to pay to have it junked. But that didn't matter to Dad. He made sure I didn't take anything with me but a suitcase. I felt bad about the coins, especially, but I was in love and didn't want to start any trouble. I wanted Dad to be happy, too.

"Charlie was the perfect husband. We loved to be together. He taught me how to hunt and fish. We even went trapping together. I wasn't good at the hunting, but I liked the fishing and trapping. We used to talk a lot about God and the angels and saints. We went to church pretty regularly and tried to pray every night before we went to bed.

"At first, I was expecting that Charlie'd be demanding like my dad was, so I always had the house superclean and always made a great dinner. But Charlie wasn't like Dad at all. He wasn't a bully. He was kind. He was articulate. He was always thoughtful of other people. He even opened the doors for me. Mom told me to watch out because the nice ones could be killers in disguise. But she didn't know Charlie. I did.

"Ya know, I actually couldn't believe I'd picked such a good guy, ya know, after what my mom had told me and all, saying that I'd never be able to get any guy to like me. He was really cute and I didn't have to pretend to be dumb, either.

"Charlie was very polite and concerned about my parents. He was particularly nice to my dad, making sure he showed his love for me by respecting his elders. He'd just lost his dad, so being respectful to my dad was very important to him.

"Charlie did plumbing at Dad's. Most times when we went on vacation, we'd invite Dad to come with. Mom always wanted to stay at home to get her housework done. I think she appreciated the time she had alone.

"Dad took out a five-thousand-dollar mortgage on his house and loaned it to us for a down payment on a small apartment house we wanted. We paid him back monthly at the same time we paid the mortgage on our house. But we didn't get to use the tax deduction. Dad used that himself. That was okay with us. We were never late with any of our payments.

"My husband and I rehabbed the apartments and raised the rents. My mother called me up crying when she heard we'd raised the rents. She said she wouldn't have anything to do with me anymore because I'd raised the rents on people. She thought I was money-hungry. She said I was selfish like my father and that I would stab anyone in the back for a nickel."

"But you never said anything? You never even commented?"

"No! Not me. I wasn't no troublemaker. But maybe I was a bad person. Maybe I was selfish, money-hungry. Maybe she was right."

"What about Charlie? What did he say?"

"He tended to agree with my mom. He said that maybe we were being greedy and that since my mom and dad were older, they probably knew more than we did. So, we lowered the rents.

"My father would visit us from time to time. If he was in a bad mood, he'd tell our tenants that he had bought the house for us and that we wouldn't have anything if it wasn't for him. Though that was not true, I didn't say anything because I didn't want to cause any trouble.

"The tenants started demanding more, like laundry facilities, new faucets, and stuff, and threatened to pay less rent. They said they'd mention it to my father if he came over. But it was our house in our name. I didn't think it was fair that my dad was saying that. After all, he was getting the benefit of the tax deduction. And even though we told the tenants that it was our house, they didn't seem to believe us.

"My husband said it didn't matter to him what my dad said because he and I knew the truth. Charlie said he would talk to the tenants and calm them down. He told me not to say anything or cause any trouble, to just let it be. He said, 'He's your dad. Be nice to him. Be happy he's still around. I don't have my dad around, although I wish I did.'

"Charlie and I had three children within a few years. Though we didn't plan it, our kids arrived in the exact order we hoped for: a boy, a girl, and then a boy. The first we named after Charlie. We were hoping he'd want to be a plumber, too. The girl was a tiny little moppet, cute as could be. And the youngest was a boy, just like we wanted! The little one was a charmer, big eyes and almost no hair till it started growing in blond. The girl was darling and looked like a little jewel, so we named her Jules. Little Charlie nicknamed her Duke because there was some cartoon character with a doggie friend called Duke.

"When they were still real small, we put all three kids on the BSA with us. Yep, we did."

"Omigosh! What were you thinking? How'd you even do that?"

"Well, Little Charlie sat on the gas tank. Jules sat between me and her dad on the seat, and the baby was in my husband's rucksack from his Army days. I put it on like a backpack so the baby could peek out. Sometimes, Jules took a turn and rode in the backpack."

"I can't even imagine how irresponsible! How could you? Did you realize what could have happened if—"

"Shut up! I told you I was just bad, a bad mother. And, well, things were different then. And I don't have to explain nothing to you, anyway. Don't even know you no more. Plus, one thing I learned from my dad: Rules were for everyone else, not us!"

"Thank God no one got hurt!"

"God, yeah, thank God no one got hurt. But later, He'd make me pay, alright—make you pay. He always gets what He wants. Anyway, the youngest one was a feisty blond-haired boy. We named him after my dad. This little boy had lots of talent. He had a little temper, but he was so lovable. I thought he'd become an artist or writer. That boy, my baby, was very creative. He loved to draw and make up his own comic strips. His stories were so cute that I found myself laughing out loud as I read them. I still have some in my backpack. I'll show them to ya later.

"He liked to swim and do funny tricks in the pool. He tried to do bicycle tricks, jumping over ramps like Evel Knievel. He loved to watch *Dukes of Hazzard*. We even called him Bo, like Bo Duke, for a time. He was a whirlwind, full of life and mischief. We didn't think that spanking was good discipline, but once in a while, a slap on the butt was necessary. Me, I did a lot of yelling. That was mostly what I did. Sometimes, I even threw pots and pans out of the cabinet, just to make a lot of noise and show that I was mad. That wasn't very effective, but that was all I knew how to do, yell and scream, just like my folks did.

"Charlie and I weren't sure about the right kind of discipline, so we went to a child psychologist. She told us about timeouts and things like that. So, we followed those suggestions and tried to reason with the kids when they did something wrong. My dad came over to visit a lot. He kept saying that we were letting the kids take over and should start doling out some real punishments like the ones he got when he was a kid. He said it so much that Charlie and I began questioning our competency as parents.

"My dad was particularly critical of the youngest son, the one we named for him. He called him 'sissy' a lot. After a time, I thought we shouldn't have named the boy after my dad. It might have been a bad idea. Although it's not easy to think this, my dad didn't seem to like him. He was always teasing and making fun of him."

"Why on earth did you let that continue? Don't you know how bad—"

"Don't you start in on me now or I'll kick you so hard you'll have boot marks on your face for the rest of your miserable life! Shut up!"

After a few minutes, the young woman calmed down and spoke a little more softly. "I didn't want to cause any trouble, that's why! I didn't say anything about it. I closed my eyes and ears. After all, you know, I was taught to listen to my parents. They knew everything, you know. And don't you tell me what I should've done! Think about what you should have done. If I get aggravated at you now, you'll never hear another word from me! I'll leave you here so deep in this place that you'll never figure out how to get out. So, don't you say *anything*! Don't *you* cause me any trouble!"

"Don't say anything? Don't cause any trouble? Didn't you understand that if you never stood up for anything that was right, you—"

"That's rich! *You're* telling *me* to stand up for what's right? Listen. You think you could have done better at that time? Did you?"

"What do you mean did I?"

"Shut up and listen. Maybe you'll finally get it, stupid."

"Okay, okay. Sorry."

"You should be sorry. You're a sorry case! Who are you to criticize me? You're the one … Oh, never mind. You'll find out."

"I said I was sorry."

"Yeah, well, keep your trap shut."

After a few minutes of silence, the woman continued speaking. She said, "One time, the two boys were dancing with my daughter by the old television set. They were just little. Those old televisions were heavy. It fell over and nicked my daughter, causing quite a scrape on her face. I got all nervous and stuff. I called Mom to watch the other kids so I could get my daughter to the hospital. It looked like Jules needed a couple of stitches.

"My mom came over and yelled that I had no right to even have any kids. She grabbed my daughter, Jules, and took her to the hospital. I didn't even know which hospital she took Jules to. I found myself calling the hospitals to check if my daughter was there and see how she was doing. The nurses at the hospital asked me why I hadn't brought her in. They said that since my mother had brought her in, I'd have to find out from her. I felt helpless. I guess it was my fault somehow.

"I ... I really was a bad mom. Even the hospital knew it. I didn't even deserve to know about my own daughter's health. I don't know; I just don't know ..."

The young woman put her head in her hands and was quiet. She guzzled more wine. "But one thing I know. All bad moms need another drink! To the bad moms of the world, a toast! Funny, though, no matter how much I drink, I can't paint prettier pictures of the stories I'm telling you. I want to make them sound good. I want to make myself sound like I was a good person. But I wasn't. I was a monster. But I guess that's why they make booze! It's good for the complexion. Okay, so, what's next?

"Anyway, my mother took my daughter to her house to stay for a day or so, saying that she could take better care of her. My dad continued visiting and would sit and talk with my husband. He again told us that the TV wouldn't have fallen if those boys had known a little harsher discipline. 'The belt, or a pitta, that's what they need. I wish I still had that pitta. I'd teach them a lesson if you're too afraid,' he'd say.

"Charlie and my dad would have a few beers, and then my dad would start asking Charlie how the 'old nag' was. I was the old nag. I complained to my husband, but he said I was making something out of nothing. He said my dad didn't have any bad intentions, that he was just having a little fun. I was taking things too seriously, my husband said.

"When we went on trips to Wisconsin, Dad would go with. We paid his way on all those trips. We took him to Mexico a couple of times and paid his way then, too. When my husband's mother died, my dad went down to Florida with us to see what she had left in their house—to see if there was anything Dad wanted.

"Many times on the trips, I caught my dad making fun of my youngest, calling him 'girlie' because he had long blond hair and making him cry. My dad would laugh, take my child's toys, and make him cry. Then, my dad would mimic his crying and cause him even more tears. I saw it but said nothing! Nothing! You know why? It was because I was afraid to cause trouble. I think that's why I'm stuck here in this swamp, because I never protected him. I never protected him, you understand?" She was screaming, almost hysterical.

"I think you're being too hard on yourself," I said.

"I'm worthless, and you, you don't know nuthin'. Don't you go trying to patronize me. It gets worse, listen. One time, my dad was in our house and began talking about our kids, how they were spoiled brats and how he wouldn't give them anything. He never gave 'em nothin' for their birthdays or Christmas, anyway, so I don't even know why he was complaining. Of his namesake, he said, 'I just can't stand that kid.'

"Again, I said nothing! My son heard that. He cried. What kind of parent would let that happen? Let her child be bullied by someone just 'cause she didn't want to say anything or cause trouble? I'll tell you what kind. The kind who lives in this godforsaken swamp! I'm no good, and I never was. I belong here." The young woman started crying. "I deserve what I got. This place, this— What're you lookin' at?"

She was embarrassed that I'd seen her cry, so I turned. She stopped crying.

"Don't feel pity for me. I got what I settled for. There's those that are cruel and those that are weak, and the weak are fodder for the bullies. That's just the way it is. Hey, that's a pun, kind of. My fodder was da bully. Ha! I learnt that from my mom, yeah. My mom let herself get bullied a lot.

"One day, my dad got a flat tire. He called my mom to bring him another tire and a tire iron. My mom didn't know a tire iron from a hammer, and it was hard for her to lift the tire. It was just too darn heavy. I don't know how she did it, but she managed to take it over to my dad.

"When she got there, he was mad that he'd had to wait so long for her. He told her to get the tire out of the trunk and bring it to him. She did. But then when he asked her to get him another tool, she picked up the wrong one. He got so mad that he punched her in the stomach. She started to cry, so he yelled at her to go home. When he got home, he was still mad at her. He never mentioned anything about being sorry that he punched her. But I saw that she had a bruise where he hit her.

"Around that time, Janet met a successful man, Keith, who was in politics. He asked her to marry him, and she said yes. My dad was beside himself with joy. He couldn't believe that one of his kids was good enough for a politician to want to marry. I remember him commenting to Keith, 'She must be really good in bed for someone like you to want to marry her.' I don't know if Janet heard that or not, but it didn't seem appropriate to say something like that to the man who was going to marry his daughter.

"After Janet and Keith got married, Dad, hoping for some special favors from Keith, treated Janet a little nicer than the rest of us. Not much had changed through the years.

"One day, my mom found out that she had cancer. They said she wouldn't last more than a year. She went for chemotherapy. It was mostly my sisters who took her for treatments. Dad complained that there was no one to make his meals and that the house wasn't clean. He complained that he had no one to talk with because my mom was sick most of the time. He was still working on the truck and said he couldn't take off any time to help out.

"After some treatments, Mom went into remission. She asked Dad to take her to Disneyland to celebrate. But, no, he said that was too much money, that he had all his money tied up in stocks.

"Less than a year later, my mom died. My sisters planned the funeral. I think my dad paid for it. But I know my sisters paid for some of the extras. Mom may have had some insurance. I don't really know, maybe my dad had an insurance policy on her because he pretty much stopped working shortly after she was gone.

"At that time, one of our acquaintances owned a flower shop. I was able to get a better price if we all ordered our flowers from them. So, I volunteered to order everyone's flowers. They all promised to pay me back. My dad placed his order. He wanted a large spray of red roses and a sign that said 'Loving Wife.' I picked the best arrangement they had and signed his name to the card.

"His flowers were around two hundred dollars. When I gave him the bill, he said that I had plenty of money and should be able to afford to pay the bill. He told me that that was the least I could do for my mother. I told him that we'd bought flowers from our family and that the roses had been from him. I told him that Charlie and I didn't have a lot of money and that everyone else had paid me for the flowers they'd ordered. He accused me of making a deal with the florist to make money off my mother's death. He never paid me for the roses. But I didn't say anything. I didn't want to cause any trouble.

"After Mom was gone, Dad wanted to stay with us. He said he couldn't stay in his house alone because he was lonely. He said he'd keep his house but didn't want to be there alone. My husband and I agreed to let him stay a while. It was not bad at first, because we were all so sad. We needed each other.

"At Christmas, my dad asked me if he should get everyone presents like my mom had done. I told him yes, that that would be the right thing to do. I volunteered to shop for him. When he asked me how much he should spend on each of us, I told him about fifty or seventy-five dollars. When he multiplied that by the seven of us, not counting our spouses, he said he'd get something for each of us on his own. I thought maybe that was a nicer way to work it. His gifts would be more heartfelt if he picked each one out.

"So, Christmas came. Dad's gift to everyone was the same, one combination lint brush/shoehorn for each family and nothing for the grand kids. You know, I still got that lint brush, saved it as a souvenir. Only gift he ever gave me besides a few bottles of cheap wine here and there—and I drank those pretty quick. He never bought me any Scotch, though, too expensive."

"Didn't you talk with any of your sisters or brothers about this?" I asked.

"Nah, even though I thought he was a cheapskate, I knew they didn't like me, so I just let it go. They'd just think I was after his money. Don't say anything, don't cause any trouble. That was my motto."

"But how do you know they didn't like you?"

"Haven't you been listening? My *dad* told me that. He told me they were all laughing at me, making fun of my kids and all."

"But knowing your dad, did you really think that was true?"

"At that time, yeah, I did. I figured it had to be true. You know, fathers don't lie, do they? Ahhh, maybe I was just kiddin' myself. I don't know. I was so stupid. Still am.

"After Dad was with us a few weeks, he started calling me 'old nag' again and singing, 'The old gray mare just ain't what she used to be,' trying to make Charlie join in and make fun of me.

"I began to notice a change in the way Charlie treated me. He began to treat me with some disrespect, but it wasn't really noticeable at first. But then, he began arguing with the kids, giving them more unnecessary rules and criticizing their behavior and their school projects. And sometimes, he spanked them pretty hard. My dad loved to get in on those arguments, siding with Charlie and ridiculing my comments.

"Many times, I tried to divert the negativity that was present in all our discussions. I'd try to bring up funny anecdotes or tell a pleasant story I'd heard on the news. One time, we were all at the table, and I told everyone a wonderful story about Jesus that I'd heard on the radio. It was about a boy who had a dream that he went to heaven and walked into a file room. There, he saw a man pull out all these cards. On each card was written a sin the boy had committed. The boy was ashamed and turned away. The man took out each card and signed his name on it. He turned to the boy, and the boy saw the name Jesus written in blood across each card. The boy cried, and the man, who was Jesus, embraced him. That's the best I remembered that story. I thought it was a great story. And sometimes, I'd put on those old songs Grandma used to sing, like 'I Believe' and 'He.' But my dad said he didn't want to hear that funeral music.

"And then my dad started saying that I was telling him he was going to die and that I was trying to make fun of him because he was old. He got mad and walked out, didn't come back until late at night.

"Charlie said I shouldn't tell any stories like that to my dad so he wouldn't feel bad. He also told me to put on some of the music that my dad liked. At first, I didn't want to say anything, didn't want to cause any trouble. But then I realized that something had to be done. The level of stress in our household was rising rapidly. I couldn't talk about God in my own house? But maybe that's how it should've been, I thought. I never heard my mom and dad talk about God. Maybe that's how adults should be, I thought. Maybe only kids talk about God. Anyway, why would I want to talk about God? He didn't seem to be there for me. I decided to stop saying grace with the family before meals. It sounded too phony.

"Our family was coming apart. Charlie was starting to act like my dad. The kids were always being punished because my dad said they needed more discipline. 'They were spoiled,' he said."

"My dad said we were spoiled, too," I said.

"Really? Well, history does have a way of repeating itself."

"If you let it," I mumbled as I pondered her comment, "If you let it."

"What was that?"

The young woman seemed irritated by the interruption, so I immediately retracted my comment. "Nothing, never mind."

"Good, 'cause I don't like being interrupted; to continue: in the evenings, Dad would take my husband to a bar with him and not tell me. They'd just up and leave. When I would ask where they were going, I'd hear my dad tell Charlie to tell me it was none of my business. When I'd complain, he'd tell my husband I was just getting hysterical like my mother. He'd laugh and say, 'She's probably on the rag. Let's just get out of here.' That would get me really mad because it was insulting, a comment made just to ridicule me. Charlie would laugh, too, and say that I was hysterical just like my mother was.

"I was always taught not to talk back to Dad, to let him do what he wanted, because, after all, he was my dad. Ever hear the phrase 'Honor thy father'? Well, with my father, it was more like 'Be a slave to thy father.' My husband, and actually me, too, while trying to be nice to my dad, were unknowingly breaking down our own family. I punished the kids simply because my dad told me to. Who was I, anyway? I was not happy, not cool, and, for sure, not nice. Was I acting hysterical? Was I really overreacting to things? Maybe I was the problem.

"Charlie and my dad weren't going to change. I was the one who had to change. I was the one who had to relax and chill out. As for God, this was none of His business. I could tell that even the mention of His name was trouble in my house. He couldn't do anything for me. I realized I'd have to find happiness and peace on my own."

Ruthlis, 1980

The young woman with the motorcycle continued talking. She said, "How could I find this happiness and peace? I decided that maybe Charlie and my dad were right. Maybe I couldn't see things from their viewpoint. I'd never be able to understand unless I was drinking, too. I wasn't being fair to them. That what adults do, drink, I thought. Why was I being so prudish? What was I afraid of?

"I figured that if I had a few drinks, it would become clear to me that there was nothing wrong. I'd also be more understanding if I started drinking—you know, be on the same level, more mellow. Then I could understand that what they were saying wasn't so bad. After all, maybe they were just having a little fun. I figured, if you can't beat them, join them. I wanted to have fun too.

"Scotch and wine became my good buddies. But what started out okay with a drink here and there quickly turned rough when I hit the class-five rapids on Whiskey River. 'Nother slug?" she asked.

I shook my head no.

"Anyway, it was okay for a while. I tried to ignore the conflict. But I couldn't drink enough not to see what was happening. It was like Charlie and me were always arguing. My dad would watch and laugh at us. He'd always take Charlie's side and then tell him, 'Let's get out of here.' And they'd leave to go to a bar or drive somewhere. I couldn't take any more. I drank more but still couldn't dull the stress or hide the problems. But the alcohol did give me more courage to be boisterous and negative and vulgar. And I sure liked yelling and swearing at Charlie and the kids. I'm sure that pleased my dad, made him real happy to see me acting just like him.

"After several months, my liquid courage gave me the ability to tell my dad that he'd have to move back home. I assured him we'd visit and said that all the other kids he had wanted him to visit, too.

"He left reluctantly and, for a while, stayed with another sister. About six months after my mom died, Dad found a girlfriend, Millie. He bragged about how great her kids were and how much money they made.

"Dad went on frequent trips with Millie. They went to Europe, several cruises, lots of states, and Disneyland. I remembered how my mom had longed to see Disneyland, and I felt bad. I reminded Dad about that and asked why he'd never taken Mom. My dad said he couldn't afford two people to go at that time. He said if my mom had been working and had been making enough money to pay for herself, then they would've gone. But she never made any money. 'She never worked a day in her life. She didn't know what it meant to work,' he said. With Millie, he had to pay only for one, himself. Millie always paid her own way. That's why he could afford to go.

"On most weekends, Dad stayed at Millie's house. Sometimes, she stayed at his house. They were friends like this for many years, but she never included us in any of her family events. She invited all of us over only once, to a party for my dad's birthday. My dad introduced my brother Jack to one of her sons who owned a mechanic shop. Dad boasted about him to Jack, saying, 'Now here's a guy who made something out of himself. You should take some lessons from him. He knows how to run a business.'

"Jack already knew how to run a business. He'd started his own business from nothing. His business was very successful, but my dad never mentioned that. He made my brother look foolish. Millie's son offered to give Jack information on how to be a successful businessman. Jack said nothing. I said nothing and ordered another Scotch. Nothing … Don't say nothing … nothin'. Just shut up and don't cause no trouble. That was us.

"The years flew by, and suddenly my babies were all grown up. I had been too interested in myself to see their needs. I'm sorry to say that I didn't encourage them to further their schooling. We had time to take trips as a family but spent it my dad instead. Money that could have been spent on our kids was spent on good ol' Dad. I was too busy trying to please my dad to see things any other way."

"This same thing happened to me!" I said. "Are you … are you me? Are you my past? It's impossible. You couldn't be me."

"Impossible, yeah, you're too good to be me. But as I said, honey, that's for me to know … and for you to find out."

I hated the tune she sang with that! I hated her! *What a wasted life,* I thought.

"So, you wanna listen, or do I start this bike up and leave?"

"I'm listening. I'm listening."

"So, how it goes is this: I should have known better, should have done better. I neglected my family and almost lost them all. More time wasted. More time wasted. Never wasted none of dis, though!" She tried to take a drink, but the bottle was empty. "Oh, nuts!" She wiped her hand across her mouth and tossed the empty bottle into the woods.

"How can you just throw your garbage in the—"

"Hey! Don't you go tellin' me what I can and can't do! I'm fed up with you, so now you got enough info from me. I'm going to head back. That's it with you. I'm just a little sick of your interruptions and criticisms."

"But you never gave me the answers I needed. You didn't help me with what I need to know. We can't be done talking," I said. "I need to know more. Didn't you pray? Didn't you ask God to help you?"

She wasn't listening. She was fishing around in the saddlebags for something. "Yeah, actually, yeah, just now, I asked Him to help me find this! It's a miracle! Thank you, God!" She pulled out a bottle of wine and took a gulp.

"You don't mock God like that! You don't—" I stopped midsentence when I heard a small noise and looked up. There, a little distance away, I saw a snowy white owl. The young woman saw me looking at it.

"Been there for a bit of time now, surprised you just noticed him. Okay, I'm almost out of time, got to get going. Hop on. I'll ride on the back. We can talk while we ride. I'm too swacked to drive, you know. Not that it would make any difference to you."

"It would make a difference to me. And I don't know how to drive a bike."

"No, it wouldn't, and yes, you do. Those are the answers to your questions, my dear! Get on the bike now! We don't have much time."

I heard loud thunder. I looked up. The owl appeared startled by the sound and was preparing to fly off. Cold wind blew across my face.

"Don't worry. We'll be okay," the woman said.

I gingerly wrapped my legs around the bike and felt for the pedals. It seemed familiar, "Which way?"

"We'll just follow him. Looks like he knows where he's going." She pointed to the snowy owl riding the wind currents overhead and then put on her helmet and hopped on the backseat. "I'll talk. You listen," she said.

"Yes, I know the rules," I said.

"Smart girl you are! It'll take a while, but we have the time if you listen to me."

"I can't see! I don't know the way!"

"Because you don't want to know the way, you puke-head, follow him. The path is bright around him. Now, drive, stupid, before he's gone and it's too late. Go!"

I jumped the pedal, started the bike, and drove into the wind. But how had I known how to start the bike? "I know you now. I know who you are," I said to my companion.

"You may know who I am, but you don't know me. You're better off letting me finish what I started. I don't think you'll be able to do this on your own. Some things you may not be able to see, and you could get lost in here pretty fast.

"So, you want to know if I asked God what to do. Okay, I tried. One day, my daughter, Jules, who had just turned eighteen, came home to tell us she'd joined the Army. I couldn't blame her for wanting to get out of the house, but I can't tell you what a shock that was! Right out of high school and into the Army! Told us she was leaving in two days. But she was eighteen. We'd had no input into her decision. She never even discussed it with us. But anyway, in two days, she left for boot camp.

"We missed her presence in the house. To me, she was still that little moppet playing with dolls. But now she was all grown up. We went to visit her when she graduated from boot camp. Charlie and I were very proud of her. My little girl, from dressing her dolls to loading guns. She became a sharpshooter.

"After a year or so, she met a nice young man from the Army and wanted to get married. She asked me to help her with the plans. She had some ideas about the songs she wanted to use in the ceremony. She wanted one of her friends to do the singing. She had some unique vows all written out, wanting her wedding to be very special. I told her that we should confer with the priest and let him know her plans.

"But when we did, he told her that she could only use the singer the church had approved for the wedding services and that there were only certain songs allowed. The priest also said that the vows were the vows written into the service. Jules couldn't change or add anything to them. He also stressed the idea of the flowers and told her where we should buy them. He insisted that we buy them from one certain flower shop. 'I've seen many a wedding ruined due to bad flowers,' he'd told her. Now, what kind of stupid remark was that? Flowers, who cares about the flowers? My daughter was a little rebellious and got them somewhere else. I think that got the priest kind of mad. He never suggested any conferences with her or her future husband."

"But I was asking how God was in or out of your life at that time. I think you're going off the subject entirely," I said.

"Hold your horses! I've been here all this time waiting for you, and now *you* are in a big old hurry."

"What do you mean you've been waiting for me?"

"Don't be stupid. You can stop pretending to be dumb. Mother isn't watching, and there aren't any boys to impress. But then, after all, you're not pretending, are you?" She paused and laughed. Before I had a chance to comment, she continued. "So, as I was saying, the wedding, the party, all came and went too quickly. Then, Jules was off living in another state. My oldest son, Little Charlie (who wasn't little anymore), moved out and bought his own house. He wasn't married at that time. Shortly after he bought the house, he got Hodgkin's disease. The doctors didn't have much hope. He was in the last stages, which were showing up as first stages. The doctors weren't sure that chemo would help him because he had inoperable tumors in his lungs. We almost lost him. He went down from a hundred and ninety pounds to a hundred and twenty. He said the pain was so bad that he wanted to die. We prayed."

"So, you did ask God for help. You believed that only He could have helped you!"

"Yeah, after a fashion, you know, a dozen rosaries and a few donations to the church. Anyway, I couldn't comprehend anything really bad happening to my family. I figured with all the church stuff I'd done when I was a kid, I'd never suffer any loss or anything like that. Not only that, but also my good buddy Cutty Sark kept me pretty mellow.

"But He did answer your prayers. He was there for you. But if He answered you, why wouldn't He answer me?"

"You mean Cutty Sark, was he there to answer me? Ha, no, of course, you don't. So, shut up, will ya? Why wouldn't God answer you? I ain't God. I'll be glad to kill ya so you can go ask Him yourself. Now, shut up or I will."

She was starting to slur her words quite a bit, so I kept quiet.

"After a year of treatments and chemotherapy, Little Charlie, or Young Charlie as we began calling him, was back with us, in remission. As soon as we found out he was in remission, he wanted to work with us. He was in his car on the way to pick up some supplies when he got hit by an express train. The train cut the car in half, sending it flying a few hundred feet into a tree. Young Charlie was ejected from the car and thrown onto a tree another hundred feet away. When the ambulance found him, he had no life signs. They were able to revive him in the ambulance.

"But if they were able to revive him, then why couldn't ..." I stopped talking and ducked as she clenched her hand in a fist and tried to punch me.

"Don't interrupt me," she said. "We rushed to the hospital. The doctors told us that his prognosis was not good. They said he'd probably be unable to even feed himself. They didn't expect him to walk or even talk again. The trauma was that bad. I was in shock. He just got over Hodgkin's, and now this."

"That must have been a sobering experience."

"Oh no, I just drank more. It was a bad time, and I needed comforting."

"I didn't mean that kind of sobering."

"Yeah, well, I don't know the kind of sobering you're talking about. We took Charlie home and watched him day and night. We had to hire a nurse to be with him every minute. His therapy was long and difficult. To the surprise of the doctors, he seemed to be showing signs of improvement.

"Months later, young Charlie was able to walk again on his own. It really was a miracle. One day, he asked me if he could take a little walk in the front by himself. I was baking cookies. The big window overlooked the front, so I told him to stay where I could watch him. As he was heading out, he said, 'Mom, I know you worry about Grandma. But you don't have to. She's very happy. I don't know why, but I just know we have to be very good to each other.'

"I got goose bumps hearing him talk like that, because I'd never verbalized any concern about my mother. After she'd died, I didn't even talk about her in front of the kids because I didn't want them to feel bad. I think something happened to my son after the train hit him. I think maybe he may have crossed over and saw something. I think Jesus gave him a glimpse of heaven."

"Amazing. Was that true?"

"Oh yeah. I just ain't got no proof of anything. He couldn't recall anything else, even though I asked him many times over the years. And whaddya mean, 'Was that true?' Am I a liar? Is this just a waste of time being here with you? I wonder."

"I'm sorry."

"Yeah, he's healthy and strong now, and he partners with his dad in the business."

"So, Jesus was there with you even in those hard times?"

"Yeah, it seemed He was. I thanked Him, but I just put Him back on the shelf with my other statues. Put back the genie in the bottle. You see, there was nothing else I knew to say to or do with Him. He was there to call on if I needed something. Just say the magic words, 'Our Father' or 'Hail Mary,' and give up a few donuts here and there. That was the extent of my interaction with God. Nothing else left to say."

"But you called on Him when you needed Him?"

"Yeah, like I said, a genie in a bottle. But not this bottle; this bottle, I'm drinking. Still, I wanted to know if there was more to learn about God. I thought there should be more I could know, more I could do, not just new prayers to memorize. Like, for instance, how does God fit into today's world? How could He help me with my lifetime questions? How could he help me with the problems with my dad, or would he just say, 'Honor thy father and mother, and keep taking the abuse'? How could He have helped me raise my kids? Was He only for Sundays? Do you go to church every Sunday, and then on Monday it's back to being an old meanie? And what would God know about marriage and raising kids? I wanted answers, and I wanted to know what else there was to know about Him. I knew heaven was there, alright, but I didn't figure it was for me. I didn't want to leave the world behind and be a nun. Heavens no! No drinking in the convents, you know.

"I didn't just want to go through the motions, those religious rituals. I mean, like, how many rosaries can you say in a lifetime? What's the use? You just hurry to finish and add another notch to your belt. I think I may hold the world's record for rosary recitation. And that's all any of those prayers were, recitations. I could recite 'em all while I was out drinking and dancing. How many are you supposed to say before you get 'enlightened'?"

"No one else in your family had any advice to offer you?" I asked.

"Yeah, well, I had three aunties, my dad's sisters. They were real holy rollers, as my mom would have said—you know fanatics! They were always saying things like 'Praise the Lord' and 'Thank you, Jesus, thank you, Jesus.' But I couldn't see what the thank-yous were for, and I certainly didn't have anything to thank Him for. It's not like I'd won the lottery or gotten a free car or anything. I didn't even have a stress-free life, so I couldn't think of anything to thank Jesus for. Well, unless someone bought me a drink. But none of them Jesus fanatics ever offered to buy me a drink!

"Anyway, Aunt June invited us to her church and took us out for food. We liked the food, and we liked the church. It was pretty informal, and the people were really friendly. But one of the problems was that I was Catholic and had always been taught that it was a mortal sin to go to a non-Catholic service, since your soul could be damned to hell. I was stupid and had too many strikes against me already. I couldn't take chance spending eternity in hell, so I didn't go to that church too many times. But Aunt June and her husband were persistent and gave me some tapes, yeah, tapes, old stuff. Used to have a tape deck in my car."

"Tape deck?"

"Yeah, you hockey puck! A tape deck! Had a great car, too, nice red Mustang convertible with plates that said 'RUTHLIS' I really meant ruthless but the correct spelling wouldn't fit on the plates. Yep, that was how I wanted to be known, as a person from the dark side, an outlaw, a tough, mean, ruthless person. I was no sad-sack female."

"What kind of tapes were they?"

"Oh yeah, the tapes. They gave me tapes that had great sermons, stuff from the Bible with messages that seemed interesting. They gave me books. But I wasn't sure they held any meaning for me. Guys like Erwin Lutzer, Tony Evans, and another guy, Lee Strobel, who was an atheist who'd converted to Christianity. I loved to read, and it seemed I read all the Stephen King and Ann Rule books. I was getting tired of true-crime books, too. Since I needed to find something else to read, I grabbed up whatever sounded interesting—and this stuff sounded pretty interesting. I was hooked.

"I think the first one I read was *The Case for Christ* by that Strobel guy. He's a lawyer, and I really like lawyers. They search under mountains of garbage to find the truth. You can't pull one over on a lawyer, you know!

"A new truth hit me. I didn't really realize there was reasoning beyond belief alone. 'Reason to Believe': sounds like a Rod Stewart song, but I didn't want to be distracted with the song. I know it sounds funny, but I actually thought I knew all this stuff but I never knew why. I think these people really had something to say that I could apply to my life. When I didn't have time to read, I listened to the tapes. I heard some stuff on them that I really liked. It was even more interesting than listening to music.

"Lots of it was about everybody else and how they should change—a lot of bad guys out there. But there were a few things that could help me, too, I thought. The aunties gave me at least one tape a week. Boy, they were persistent. But I'm kinda glad they were.

"About that time, my youngest son, little blondie, came to me and told me he wanted to leave Wisconsin. I was very surprised. I didn't want him to go, but he was over twenty-one. I knew I couldn't hold him home forever. He'd graduated from college and wanted to make a mark on the world. He was very creative. He wanted to get into the entertainment business. He'd done some acting and scripted some plays in Wisconsin, but he felt he'd have more opportunities in California.

"One of the most unique things he did was different voices. He could change his voice into different dialects and characters in an instant. There were a few cartoon auditions he planned to go to. I couldn't hold him back from what he really wanted to do. And I wanted him to be happy. My heart was breaking as he went about packing his stuff. I tried to talk him out of it even though I knew he had to do what was in his heart.

"I remember tears falling from my eyes as his little red pickup rounded the corner and headed off to parts unknown. Where was Jesus then? Not there to convince him to stay with us. Not there to give me any comfort. I was proud of my boy's independence, but I was worried. We didn't know anyone in California, and it was a long way to drive alone. But he promised to call me most every day to let me know he was alright. He kept his promise.

"After he found a little place to rent, he told me he was going to legally change his first name to Justin. When I asked him why, he told me he had heard what my dad had said about him: 'I just can't stand that kid.'

"I said, 'Oh no, he didn't say anything like that.' I lied my very best lie.

"'I heard it, Mom,' he told me. 'I heard him say it when he was in the kitchen talking to you and Dad.' I had to agree with him and tell the truth."

"You're me, me in the past, aren't you? But how?" I asked.

"Not now, not yet. You'll know when the time is right. Let it go for now. My son began taking small acting jobs and doing some commercials. To help pay the rent, he did some handyman work and took some painting jobs. He signed up to do a play called *Tony and Tina's Wedding*. That was a move that changed his life forever.

"He didn't tell me right away, but that's when he met the love of his life, a petite longhair who was smart and a surfer—the whole California thing. Wow, he was hooked. I never saw him so crazy about someone as he was about this gal. Sarah was her name. He told me he wasn't coming back to Wisconsin to live because he knew he'd spend the rest of his life with her in California. That was even before they started dating! I was happy for him, even though I wanted him near us.

"Still, he called almost every day. My husband and I waited anxiously for the day when Justin would bring Sarah home to meet us. There were times when he'd call up to play little pranks on me. Sometimes, I didn't even recognize his voice, like the time he pretended to be a policeman. One time when we talked, I told him about an incident with his dad, mentioning that when he sat down at a restaurant, his butt crack showed. Well, Charlie was a plumber and couldn't help it, I guess. But it was really obvious. So, I told Justin about it, and we laughed. Later, Justin called and, using one of his funny voices, left a message on our machine. He said he was a policeman and that he had a signed complaint from the restaurant owner, who was pressing charges. The 'policeman' said that it was a felony to show your butt crack in a restaurant, so he was coming over with a warrant for Charlie's arrest. Charlie really believed it! He was rehearsing what he would say to the policeman when I cracked up laughing. He told me to stop laughing, that this was a serious thing.

"When I told him that it was really Justin, he could hardly believe it! He had to listen to the message over and over to make sure. He didn't even recognize his own son's voice. Justin and I had a good laugh about that.

"One day, Justin brought his girlfriend home. We were so excited. It was a special event for all of us. When we met Sarah, we knew they'd be together forever, in love forever. She was so thoughtful of him. You could see it in her eyes. And when they were together, they saw no one else but each other.

"Justin was very thoughtful of other people. When we bought him a computer for Christmas, he cried. He was happy about it, but he knew we didn't have enough money. He was concerned that we'd spent so much on him.

"He wanted to make everyone happy. He wanted to be liked, not worshiped—just liked and respected. Though he tried to please everyone, it really bothered him that one of his neighbors didn't like him. I told him to just try to be nice, not to say anything and not to start any trouble. But each time he visited us, he told us about what the neighbor was doing—throwing his wet laundry out of the machine and onto the floor, putting threatening notes under his door, stopping the elevator, and more.

"This wasn't a neighbor. This was something evil, something that lived on sucking the joy from others. I didn't fully understand what it was until it was too late. Foolishly, I assured him that everything would be alright. I prayed for him every time he went home.

"Each time we took them to the airport, we tried to give him a little money. He wouldn't take it. We made it a little joke. We said it was only a couple of bucks. The couple of bucks were silver dollars. He treasured them so much that he got a little book and found out what was happening in the years they were minted. He and Sarah loved to speculate about where the old dollars had been and what history they held.

"He always left with a tear in his eye, telling us how much he loved us. When Sarah and Justin went back to California, my husband and I were on our own again. *Now what?* I thought. *What comes next? Who'll tell me what to do with the rest of my life? What will become important now that the kids have moved out? What role do I play as a mother in all this?*"

Money, Money, Money, 1990

The woman with the motorcycle continued telling me her story. She said, "The one thing I remembered was what my dad said about money: that it was the most important thing in life. Stocks, dollars, precious metals—money was everything. I asked him about stocks and if he would tell me something about them, how they worked. He laughed and said that he'd had to learn it on his own. He'd made a million on his own but he lost some, too. He told me to figure it out for myself and see how it is to lose money. That was the only way I would learn, he told me. Then he actually thumbed his nose at me. He started lecturing me about how he'd made so much money on his own and no one had ever helped him. 'Every dime, every dime, I made on my own. Go out yourself and see how much money you can make. 'Nothing, you'll make nothing. None of my kids will ever have more than me,' he told me.

"Though Charlie and I didn't ask him, he told me not to count on him for any loans or money, because he wouldn't help any of his kids at all. He said, 'Don't come to me if you're dying and need a buck, 'cause you won't get it from me.' He said that from the moment we kids were born, we cost him money. He wished he would have put us all in a sack and thrown us into the river. He said we were all worthless leeches. He told me not to count on any of his money after he was gone because he'd let it go to the state so all his kids could fight over it. Or maybe he'd give it all to an animal shelter, anyone but his kids. He said he'd rather see it burn than let any of his kids get a penny of it.

"He said he really didn't care if we lived or died. He said we'd never have anything. He reminded me of how much grief all his kids caused

113

him and said that if he had it to do all over he wouldn't have had any kids at all. What a tirade he spewed just because I asked one question!

"But we figured he never really meant what he said because parents can't help but love their kids. So, we guessed that he really cared but didn't know how to show it. It seemed that the only thing my dad would respect was if one of us became a millionaire. Then, that person could shower him with money and, for sure, he'd like him or her.

"Brainwashing, I'm telling you. That's what he was doing," I said.

"Ah, go tell yourself. I'm talking now," she replied. Then she continued. "I could cook really good food, so Charlie and I bought a small restaurant. At first it was pretty successful. Then my dad told me to tell my brothers and sisters that he'd given me the money to buy the restaurant so they'd be jealous that he hadn't given them any. He said they didn't like me, anyway, and that would really drive them crazy.

"I was almost going to do it, but Charlie said that it wouldn't be right because we'd saved the money ourselves. He asked me why I'd want to make my sisters and brothers jealous. Charlie said that if they didn't like me, I should leave them alone and not aggravate them and make them jealous. He had a point, so I didn't do it. My dad got really mad about that. He ranted about how we never did anything he wanted."

"Didn't you realize you were all being brainwashed from the moment you could talk?" I asked.

"I don't even know what you're talking about. Brainwashed? I don't even know what that is. Let me finish my story. I don't have much time." After pausing for a moment, she continued. "So, I hired my sister Sadie's son, Chris, to do some work at the restaurant, but the restaurant business lasted only about a year. I couldn't keep up with the hours. I really knew nothing about that business, anyway. Our cash flow went down, and the restaurant closed. I still owed Chris about a hundred dollars. He asked me for it a couple of times, but I didn't have it. He was just starting in college and needed it. After all, he had earned it. It was very embarrassing not having the money to pay the kid. I wanted to get him his money as soon as I was able to get it together. When I finally got the money, I wanted to get the cash to him really fast.

"I knew that my dad played cards with Chris's grandfather every

Friday night. It was a standing invitation for all of us to meet there for the card game. My husband and I hadn't gone because we were ashamed that we still owed Chris this money.

"Chris's grandfather liked my husband and me, and we all got along very well. I don't think the rest of the family knew we owed Chris any money, but still, we knew and felt badly about it, so we didn't go to the card game. I knew Chris and my dad would be there playing cards that night, so I asked my dad to quietly give Chris the money and tell him how sorry I was that it was late.

"Several weeks later, Chris's grandfather stopped inviting us over and didn't answer our calls. My sister Sadie seemed very cold toward me. Charlie and I figured it was because we'd been so late in paying Chris. We felt bad.

"I found out months later what happened at that Friday night card game when Dad was supposed to give Chris his money. Everyone was drinking at that game. In front of everyone, my dad pulled out the money and threw it across the table at Chris. Dad said, 'Hey, cheapskate. Here's the money your aunt owes you. She said to tell you to go suck an egg and that she hopes you choke on the money.'

"By the time I heard about that and called to say that I'd never said that, the relationship was broken. Chris's mom, my sister Sadie; her husband; and even Chris's grandfather all thought it was a horrible thing to say to someone you owed money to. And it was. But I hadn't said it! That's not my style. If I want to tell someone off, I do it in person. And I didn't want to tell Chris off, anyway. The problem was me, not him. But the way I was, a loudmouth who was drinking and all, they all believed what my dad had said and held it against me. Nothing I said could change their minds. It was too late. I think they still believe I said that."

"But why would they? You told them the truth."

"Yeah, but they reasoned, why would a father say such a thing if it wasn't true? Fathers don't lie, do they? And Dad would just say that's what I told him to tell Chris. So, rather than address an issue from months earlier, I didn't say anything. I didn't want to cause any trouble. I just let it go. Life continued as usual. And rather than just try to get on with our lives on our own, my husband and I continued to take Dad with us almost everywhere we went. I think we were trying to convince him to like us."

"It was the brainwashing. I don't know why you cared about him after all those years of abuse."

"Wish I knew, too. Dad came over to visit us often. I always made a good supper, and there was always plenty of beer in the house. He'd park his car in our driveway. One day, my other nephew, Dale, Martha's son, was driving our truck because he was working with us to make a little extra money. He accidently backed the truck into the front end of my dad's old Buick, which was over fifteen years old and not in great shape. And I couldn't even see any damage. Well, maybe a little to the grille. But you'd have to really look to find the scratches. Dad yelled and was trying to start a big fight with Dale, threatening to punch him and all, so I told Dad that we had insurance and could pay to have his car fixed, if necessary. He said, 'You bet I want it fixed!'

"Our insurance had a thousand-dollar deductible. Dad didn't care about any deductible. He said that it was our fault and he wanted his car fixed. He said it was his favorite car of all time. Our insurance company told him to take the car to two places for estimates. He did and they gave him estimates between twelve hundred and fifteen hundred dollars. But then my dad said that he wanted to take the car to his girlfriend's son's shop and get another estimate. That was the son he'd bragged about to my brother Jack. The estimate he got from Millie's son was twenty-five hundred dollars.

"He complained to our insurance company that this was his favorite car. It had low miles. He wanted Millie's son's company to do the work because they did the best job. I told Dad that the whole car wasn't worth that amount. I knew he'd driven that car every day since he'd bought it. There had to be over a hundred thousand miles on it. But he insisted that he wanted the car fixed because it was valuable and almost in mint condition, given its low miles. We paid the deductible, and my insurance company paid him twenty-five hundred dollars. He never got the car fixed. He kept the money.

"Later, Dad bragged about how his girlfriend's son disconnected the speedometer on the Buick. I told him that that was illegal. He said that

I was stupid. He said he could sell the car for more money if it had low mileage. He said that everybody did that. I told him that I didn't think they did. He told me that if I said anything to anyone, then I'd get in trouble. I thought it was terrible, but my husband said to forget it. Don't say anything; don't start any trouble. Charlie wanted only to please my dad and it seemed so did I.

"Dad would always tell us lies about my brothers and sisters. I should've known better, but I'm ashamed to say that I believed every word he said about them. Yet it always surprised me when they believed the lies he told them about me. He'd tell me that my brother wanted my dad to sign all his money over to him. He told my sisters that I wanted him to sign all his money over to me. He told anyone who'd listen that his kids were all trying to steal his money.

"But I don't think he had that much money, anyway. I mean, it's not like he was a multi millionaire. And most of us had more than he did, anyway. But he just kept talking about his money, all the time. He told me that my sister Janet wanted to make sure none of us got to his money so that she could take it all. He said she wanted him to give it all to her husband, who would make us beg him if we needed anything. But then, he told Janet that I wanted him locked up in a rubber room so I could take all his money!

"What was the matter with me? I shouldn't have believed him. I should have seen what he was doing. We all should have seen it. So we, my brothers and sisters, grew apart, always suspicious of each other's intentions. Instead of confronting each other with the things he said, we just kept silent, not saying anything, not starting any trouble, each of us content thinking that Dad liked us best. But slowly, over time, we grew farther apart.

"If we invited our sisters or brothers over for a birthday or a party, Dad told them that we were just looking for donations. He told us that they didn't want to come over and that we were trying to make them feel obligated to send a gift even though they didn't want to. And if we didn't invite anyone, then we were snubbing them. Dad seemed to enjoy the bickering among us. Indeed, he encouraged it.

"Several years later, we heard of a terrible car accident in Illinois. A van with six children, the Willis family's, was hit by a truck and caught on fire. The accident claimed the lives of all six children. My dad talked about that accident. He said that the parents were really lucky. He said that he wished that something like that would have happened to his kids a long time ago; then, he wouldn't have had any problems with my mother or with anything else. Life would have been good. Instead, he was stuck with all of us. It made me sad to hear him say that. He didn't see us as people. He saw us as problems.

"He said things like that to the little girl, too," I said.

"Oh yeah, the little girl, evil thing, that kid, huh? Piece of stink, right?"

"Omigosh, he said that! Yes, she told me," I said.

"Lots of similarities, lots, I wanted to tell him that that was a terrible thing to say. I wanted to tell him that I'd never say that about my children. But I was great at not saying anything and not starting trouble. That was the one thing I could really do! I was depressed about being who I was. I knew I was just nobody. I think I wanted to somehow impress my dad by doing some great thing that would make him proud of me, something to validate myself as a person. I wanted to do something that would make a lot of money, something to make him like me. I knew that if I impressed him I'd be impressing Charlie and my sisters and brothers, too. Maybe they would all like me. I never stopped to think that I was a mother and a wife and that Charlie and I should be discussing a future together, some future that had nothing to do with my dad. I still saw myself as a stupid little kid, programmed to fail.

"But while I was trying to impress my dad, at the same time I realized that I didn't want to be like my dad. In my heart, I knew he was really mean and selfish, but I refused to believe that. I wanted to be like someone, someone else, not myself, because I was such a nothing. I was always impressed with how everyone, even me, seemed to want to be with my dad even though he would belittle them and swear and tell lies. Why were we all trying to impress our dad?"

"Brainwashing. I told you."

"Yeah, you may have something there. Too bad you didn't figure that out long, long ago.

"When I suggested to my sisters or brothers that the things he was doing and saying weren't right, they'd tell me, 'He's just saying that. He doesn't mean anything bad. He's just that way. He's always been that way.' But, like I told you, Dad told me that they didn't like me, anyway, so what was the use in talking with them? I started thinking that he really did mean what he said and that the truth was worse than any lie. This was consuming my life. Where could I go? Who could I see? I remembered a little Jesus statue."

I do, too, I thought. *The little First Communion Jesus.*

"Maybe I needed a little bit of God's influence in my life, just a little, just enough to let me know which way to go. But I wasn't going back to those empty services. And I couldn't go to my aunties' church because my soul would be condemned to hell. So, why wasn't God helping me out? Where were my answers? I thought I was being holy. I'd been going to church, following all the rituals, saying all the prayers. I could say five rosaries in half an hour. How holy could you get? I saw *King of Kings* on TV more than once. Charlton Heston in *Moses* showed me all I needed to know about the Bible. I knew about Christmas and Easter, so that was enough, wasn't it?

"I began to think that God, as I was thinking of God, and God's rules were just a basic outline for life, just some nice entertainment that was outdated. Maybe God wasn't the answer, after all. Maybe New Age religion is right: Light a candle, chant a few chants, and you'll find that you are God. But I could be way off. So, just in case I was wrong, I didn't want to mess up my chance of getting in good with Him.

"In the confessional, I asked a priest about my God questions. It just happened to be the same priest who had made the comment about the flowers for my daughter's wedding. But he didn't know who was asking, because, in the confessional, you're kinda hidden. So, I thought that maybe he'd tell me what was missing in my life. Maybe he could tell me what I was supposed to do or be next. Maybe he had the script for the rest of my life.

"He seemed in a big hurry. The only advice he gave me was to say more rosaries and more prayers and try to go to Mass every day. 'Pray to God, our loving and protective Father, who cares for all of us as our earthly fathers do.' Father, this guy's got to be kidding; a father like my father, my loving protecting father? Was he an example of this loving God? Wow, that's a God I don't want to know.

"I didn't see how more praying would help. I was already able to pray as fast as an auctioneer, saying a bunch of dead words that meant nothing. And I didn't think that God was getting much out of it, either. What was I supposed to do to make God's Words come alive? I didn't even know all His Words, anyway, or what they even meant.

"But I did what the priest told me to do. Yep, I just did what he said. I said more rosaries and more prayers, but I was just filling up more time, not improving at all. I thought that maybe I should see another priest, one who could give me a little more insight into why I was saying those prayers or what they really meant, but I decided to give it the benefit of the doubt and wait a little longer to see if I magically became enlightened.

"After a few months, nothing changed by my saying all those prayers, so I made an appointment with a different priest. I arrived a few minutes early. The priest wasn't there. The secretary gave me a room to sit in, where I waited and waited. I waited for two hours before the secretary came back in. 'Father Kenny just called. He won't be able to keep the meeting. He's shopping for vestments for Holy Week, and this is a very busy time for him. He said to reschedule an appointment for some time after Holy Week,' she said. I said thanks and left. It looked like there were going to be no answers from any priest. Let 'em go shopping, I figured. I could use some new shoes myself. The priests don't want me. I don't need them, anyway.

"I started to think honestly that there was no way they could help me know what was right or wrong. Plus, my small church donations didn't exactly single me out for special treatment. I'd gone knocking on a priest's door twice, and each had just blown me off twice. On one hand, they tell you that it's a blessing to be poor, to give all you have to the church, and on the other, they buy expensive designer vestments and live in castles with priceless art surrounded by gold! Shopping for vestments? Didn't they care about my soul? No way! Those guys reminded me of my dad: Money, that's what's important. I thought they were hypocrites, but I was raised not to question authority, to shut up and not cause any trouble."

She sat, looking off into space, shaking her head and chugging her wine.

"Gotta quit this one day," she said, looking at the bottle. "But not yet, not until I got this all figured out." She took another drink. "So, I just figured I'd have to find God my own way. Kind of design my own religion, you know? I had listened to a lot of Bob Dylan songs pointing out the hypocrites, who were everyone but me, of course! I listened a lot to Cat Stevens, who also seemed to be searching for something.

"Or maybe it was as simple as what Dad always said. Money will buy you happiness! Maybe money *was* the most important thing. Maybe I'd start my own company and find talent and make records like Cat Stevens and Bob Dylan. I could talk to those guys and maybe learn the answers from them. I knew nothing of how to even start, but I figured that maybe with the money Charlie and I had saved, we could buy our way into that kind of business. I had no idea how treacherous that would be. I went in as a lamb to the wolves or, I would say, more as a stupid person begging to be swindled!

"I met more than a few people who misrepresented their importance in the industry. I didn't have the education or the experience to know that. I didn't check up on any of them, and I didn't ask God for any help. So, all by myself, I met a really slick conman, the worst, Sean Boros. I don't even know if that was his real name. Though I didn't realize it at the time, it was the Devil, not God, who was guiding me.

"Sean drew up a contract with me to start my own business. It seemed like a good idea. I was to give Sean money to find and develop talent. He would procure the record deal, and we'd share the profits. He also told me to be on the lookout and find some talent, too.

"He'd had great success with a couple big-name rock stars. That much I knew was true. I never checked anything else he told me. I figured that you don't question someone in his position. He promised that we'd have a winning partnership. He insisted that I wouldn't lose any money because he had at least a couple of recording contracts pending. But every time I thought we had a deal ready to close, he told me we needed just a little more money to finalize things.

"I was hesitant. Charlie was worried about the money, too. But then, Sean said, 'Send your husband out here to meet me. He'll see I'm legit.' Charlie suggested that he take my dad with so he could give us his opinion of Sean. I was blinded by another chance to impress my dad with a trip to California so he could meet celebrities and have all his expenses paid!

"I can't believe your stupidity," I said.

"Right on … We bought Dad's ticket to Los Angeles, and he and my husband went. They talked about business with Sean, but since it wasn't a business they knew anything about, they had to depend on their ability to judge character in order to see what this guy was like. My dad was crazy about Sean. Sean introduced him and Charlie to a couple of celebrities, and then they went to a bar. My dad had the best time singing with all the patrons. My dad said that he could tell that this guy, Sean, was the real thing. Most important, Dad finally seemed to like me. He kept talking about what a wonderful trip that was and what a great guy Sean was. Even though my husband wasn't too sure about Sean, we trusted my dad's opinion. So, I felt very confident when I put most of our life savings into what seemed to be a very good investment.

"Sean urged me to find groups and make CD demos. So I did. I worked with lots of bands. I wanted to share the African music I'd heard, get it into mainstream. I worked with artists from Ethiopia, Senegal, Jamaica, and rock bands from the U.S. Some of the groups, I thought were great, but Sean wasn't able to get them any kind of record deal or even a show. This was way harder than I thought. I couldn't do it. I had no musical background and no business acumen. I had no clue as to what I was doing. I didn't realize it then, but I was just a cash cow.

"One of the bands I worked with played at Louis Farrakhan's daughter's wedding reception. At least he recognized their talent. But they didn't get that job through Sean; they got it on their own.

"A couple of the reggae bands I worked with let my son, Justin do some singing with them when they did shows. Justin was good at it. All of the guys in the band liked him, and he liked them. On downtime with them, Justin did great imitations of their Jamaican accents. They had a lot of fun laughing with him. They tried to do 'white boy' imitations, but they couldn't. It was hilarious to hear them try.

"One of the things they had fun doing was having Justin make up a reggae beat to any song they named. It was so funny. One of us would name a song, and then Justin would sing it with a reggae beat. He did it flawlessly, from Beatles songs to rap numbers, and so easily. We took turns, but when I tried, it never came out the same. We never did it onstage. It was just a real funny thing we did, and it was a good memory for me.

"So, things seemed to be going better for me. The future seemed to hold some promise. Stop the bike for a minute."

"But I don't want to lose sight of the owl. I'm following it. There's no path to see," I complained.

"You going to do what I say or what?" the young woman yelled.

I squeezed on the brakes, shifted into neutral, and idled while she got off and reached deep into one of the saddlebags.

"There. I knew I had at least one left!" She pulled out a small bottle of Jägermeister and unscrewed the cap.

"Shouldn't you not mix drinks? And how can you fit all that liquor into those bags?" I asked.

"I have an endless supply here in my bags, dear an endless supply. And not mixing drinks? That's an old wives' tale! Here. Chug it."

"I told you, I don't drink!" I said.

"How about a spliff, then? I could roll you a j if you want."

"Please, no. I don't do drugs!"

"Well, Miss Prudy, if you didn't then, you should now. Now it gets interesting!" She laughed raucously while the engine idled.

I held up my hand to say no. *How many more times will I have to say no?*

"No problem. More for me! You ain't gonna discourage me. I'll drink alone, then. But maybe that *is* the answer you're looking for. Maybe you need to drink."

"Did it help you?"

"It does for now. Don't worry! Be happy!"

She drank almost half the bottle before she screwed the cap back on. "Ah, mudder's milk!" She jumped back on the bike. "Okay, let's travel. No time to waste. Can't have you turn into a pumpkin now, can we?"

"Which way?" I asked. Then I spotted the owl in the distance. It was almost out of sight. I tried to catch up with it while she rambled on.

"Let's see. Where was I? Or where was you? Ha-ha-ha! Oh yeah. My mind's getting brighter each time I have a drink! Yeah, God, I was gonna tell you my idea about God. I had time to formulate my own idea of God, and it was much better than anyone could imagine: my own custom religion. This is great. You'll love it! He was God, Jesus, Buddha, Vishnu, and Allah all in one. He turned himself into different gods for different people. And the rules were different. It didn't matter which one you prayed to as long as you prayed to someone or something.

"I thought Santería and voodoo were a little dangerous, but I thought that parts of them could be incorporated into some of my 'New Age' religious beliefs. Heavy incense—patchouli worked particularly well—would enhance this new way of worship. I steered clear of pentagrams, psychics, and séances. A friend gave me a talisman made of black goatskin from Africa, and I wore it on a string around my neck. It was a strange piece. There was something in it, but it was sealed and I never opened it. I decided that ancient trees and rocks and some crystals had special powers. I used to carry around an old piece of bark from the oldest-known redwood. There were signs all over that read, 'Don't Touch This Tree!' But I managed to get a piece of it, anyway. Whaddya think of that?"

"Don't you pay any mind to rules at all?" I asked.

"As I said before, rules are for everyone else, not me. I make my own rules. That's how I play the game. Rules: only my own, my dear, only my own. To continue, I also thought you could use the power of your mind to control things. I'd seen *Carrie* and *Firestarter* and felt that that was something I could do. I also thought that there could be good witches and bad witches. You know, like on Wizard of Oz. One of my friends even suggested I get a license plate that said 'WICCA.' But I thought that was a little over the top, don'tcha think?"

"*You* thought that was over the top?" I asked.

"Yeah I did, so what? Start with me and I'll dump you off."

"But I'm driving!"

"Just shut up, okay? So, I was happy with that formula for a while, until I decided to put a curse on someone I was angry with. I didn't think it would really work, but it did. And the person got more than a few stiches when he fell. I immediately knew I was going too far off on my own. Once, I even saw ... and then. Well, never mind. That's just too scary to think about.

"I got scared, too. Can you believe it? Me, scared? Living in this place? Anyway, it became clear that I was heading into a downward spiral. I used to drive around hoping I'd hit a lamppost or a tree. I know now that I could have been lost completely had I not been introduced to the amazing God I never knew but thought I did. How would I ever find the real God, you ask? That's the big question, isn't it? But that day was a long way off. Meanwhile, more money was being sucked into this recording and talent-finding sham of a company I was in.

"I went into the hospital for something. I don't even remember what, to have my appendix removed or a tonsillectomy. There I met a hospital volunteer whom I got to talking with. He said he'd left a pretty successful band and was looking for something new. He gave me a tape. I told him I'd have Sean listen to it and see if he could do anything with it.

"I sent it to Sean. Sean listened and said that the guy had no talent and that anyone who'd leave a successful band had no future. He sent me back the tape. I didn't know any better.

"Later, I looked at the tape. The name on it was Perry Farrell. I'd never heard of him. I tossed it out. *No future for this untalented guy,* I thought. Later, when I found out who this guy was, I finally figured out that Sean was a phony. But it's also possible that someone claiming to be Perry Farrell gave me a tape. I was so dumb.

"Finally, when I told Sean I had no more money, he said he'd done all he could and that we should part ways. I reminded him that he'd promised me that if there were no record deals, I'd at least get my money back. He actually said, 'Tough luck. It's all gone.' I'd lost all our savings. That was more of a problem than a couple of drinks could solve.

"Charlie was really angry and figured that there was nothing we could do. My dad laughed and said, 'I knew that guy was a crook.' I finally had to admit to myself that I had been swindled. I wanted a lawyer. But I had no money for a lawyer. Charlie just hated me for losing the money. He said that no lawyer would even talk to me.

"But I remembered this one man, Rob Hannria, I'd met in California long ago. He was a lawyer, and he seemed really honest. So, I called him. Rob was the real deal, a good man, an honest man. I should have consulted with him in the first place, before I listened to Sean. He said I'd need a litigation attorney and that he would try to find someone who could help me.

"But he chastised me for being so stupid. I guess he was right. Well, I knew he was right. But Rob had such a sense of justice that he helped me find the right person to consult with. I scraped up some money for a ticket to L.A. and met with Rob's friend Sheila B. I was scared at first because Rob wasn't going to be there and I'd never met Sheila. I had to do this all by myself. Sheila agreed to meet me on a Sunday morning at her law firm.

"I brought along all the evidence I had, which was a box of canceled checks, contracts, tapes, and CDs, and emails. Sheila said the wording of the contract was so ambiguous that I must have been drunk when I signed it. Well, I couldn't argue with her on that. At first, Sheila said that there was nothing she could do to help me. But I begged her. I mentioned the rock stars that Sean had been successful with. She told me that she knew of Sean. She told me what a fool I'd been, but I already knew that. She said she'd look at my box of papers and get back to me. But she told me, 'There is no court that awards you for being stupid.'

"I left her office. The next day, I took a long walk. I came across this little church near the beach. It was open, even though it was late. I lit a candle, for which I had no money to pay. But I was ready if some priest came out to refuse me. I was ready to tell him off and light the candle anyway. No one would keep me from my own prayer. I figured that God would have wanted me to stand up for myself.

"No priest showed up. In fact, I was the only one in the church. I prayed my own little prayer and promised that I would change my life and invite God in if He would show me the way to find Him.

"Later, I found out more about that little church. It was usually locked, especially late in the day. If it wasn't locked, then there was commonly a custodian present, because the altarpieces were made of real gold. But no one was there. I was alone. That was really a special sign for me. With hope in my heart, I took a plane home.

"A few weeks later, Rob called. Sheila had reconsidered and had decided to take my case. Rob was a guardian angel. Without him, I wouldn't have been able to do anything about the situation. My dad told me that I shouldn't try to sue Sean because he'd been so nice to him when he was out in L.A. and he'd feel bad for Sean. But I told him that I had no choice, because this guy had taken all my money. My dad said it was my fault and that I deserved to lose it. His laughter still rings in my ears.

"Against all odds, we got a trial. I found a cheap hotel out there, and I walked each day to the courthouse. It was a long walk, but I didn't have cab fare. I also started praying, but not any rehearsed prayers. These were prayers I made up on my own, asking God to give me another chance, asking Him to show me the way.

"One day on my way back from court, I passed a house with hedges made of jade plants. I wanted to pick one leaf off and start my own jade plant. I knew how to do that. But something told me no, that would be stealing. And if I wanted to win my case, I'd need to obey all God's rules. One of those rules was no stealing, no matter how small a thing. I listened to the voices. The voices were real. Even though I didn't think it would be any big deal to pinch off one of the leaves, I left the hedge alone.

"A couple of days into the trial, there was a windstorm. I walked past the same hedge and saw hundreds of jade leaves on the ground. I thought it was a sign from God, letting me know that He'd seen that I'd obeyed Him and hadn't picked any. I knew then that it would be okay to pick them up, because they were all over the ground. I picked up a few and started little jade plants that I still have to this day.

"In another week, the trial was over. I'd won. I was awarded all my money back."

"That's amazing!" was all I could say.

"I went to the little church near the beach to thank God. Again, it was late; again, it was open; and again, I was the only one there. I had no money, but I lit another candle."

Encounters

"That was the sign I'd been waiting and hoping for. You know, the jade plant thing, the open church thing, no one there to make me pay for a candle. These were signs to me. I decided to keep my promise. I wanted to continue in my search for this God who seemed to be trying to communicate with me.

"I was very confused. When I got home, I didn't want to fall back into the patterns I'd been trying to escape. I didn't want to be influenced by my dad anymore, and I didn't want him to have influence over my family. I was tired of hearing that I had to honor my father and show him respect. I didn't want to take any abuse any longer. I didn't even want to talk to him. But I worried. Would that be disrespectful? How would God judge me on that?

"How would you figure out if God's Words were true? And what were His Words on all this? Which church were you supposed to go to when every church claimed to be the one and only? And most important, which church would tell you the truth? I was back to where I'd been years ago, but I was maybe a little smarter now.

"I cried out for another sign from God. I asked Him if He wanted me back or if He was just going to dump me back at the Devil's fountain. I was in my car, which still had license plates reading, 'RUTHLIS.' I was crying so much that I could hardly drive. I had a Sting song playing. The words he sang were loud: 'He won't love you like I love you. He won't care for you this way. He'll mistreat you if you stay.'

"In the song, there were some warnings about how the man was counting on buying a woman's soul. When I looked up, I saw the brightest light. I saw Jesus sitting on a throne. Angels surrounded Him. I tried to see His face, but it was too bright. All I could see was golden hair and shining rays around Him. The light was radiating all around His face, like hot sand in a desert. I knew He was smiling and I saw Him reaching out. I wanted to see His face. I wanted to remember what He looked like. But the light hurt my eyes. Not even like the sun, it was white bright, like an arc welder. My eyes burned, it was so bright. The angels were in the thousands, in soft sherbet colors. They were all pressed against each other like sardines on what looked like steps up to a throne.

"I know that this must sound wacky, but it's true. There I was in my car, stopped at a light, listening to Sting, seeing the throne of God over a golf course in a suburb in Wisconsin. I realized the he in the 'he won't love you' for me, meant the Devil and the other pronoun, I 'like I love you', stood for God."

"But was it true? Did you see this?"

"You calling me a liar again? 'Cause if you are, you can just take a hike now on your own. I just can't stand this —"

"Okay, okay. Sorry. I just—"

"Rules, remember the rules! This won't work if you don't remember the rules."

"Right, right, please go on."

"I'm not a liar, not anymore. Oh, I saw it alright, I saw it. Tears rolled down my face, and I was shaking. I wanted to stay, but I heard car horns urging me to move, so I continued on my way. But I knew what I saw, and you know I'm telling the truth."

"It seems Jesus was always there when you needed Him," I said.

"I don't know why, but I guess the answer's yes, He was, especially at that time. But I still didn't have the practical answers as to how I could make Him part of my daily life.

"Then, my daughter was having problems in her marriage. She was filing for divorce. She said she needed life answers, but I couldn't give her any. I told her I needed some of my own. She said, 'Let's go shopping for a church.' I was kinda taken aback at that. I didn't think you were allowed to just go into another church if you weren't a member. But she insisted it was alright. She told me we'd go to a different church each week and see what the messages were. We'd see what sounded real and what sounded phony. That sounded okay to me.

"We tried them out, like Goldilocks and the three bears. Some were just too big, some were too hard, and some were too soft. But we eventually found one that was just right. It was a tiny church called North Shore Assembly of God. There were lots of fanatics there. I wondered what my mother would've thought.

"There was truth that reached out to both me and my daughter. Oddly enough, it was the same kind of church my aunties had taken me to several years earlier. How far I'd traveled just to get back to there! They must have planted a seed, I guess. This was the one, I thought. It was real. My daughter knew it too. I wondered if I would turn into one of these fanatics. So, I tossed out the ancient tree bark, the goatskin necklace (never did open it, never knew what was in it), and the 'sacred' rocks I'd saved. Even got rid of my patchouli oil!

"The message of this church was simple: No one could be saved by themselves or by their own good works. I couldn't save myself by anything I did. Nothing that anyone could do was big enough to equal the sacrifice God had made by giving His Son up for our sins. No quantity of prayers or litanies to saints, no amount of sacrifices, no living in a cave, no giving up sweets for a lifetime, no good works, no huge donations, no flailing yourself with glass-coated straps, nothing would do it, nothing but faith in His Words.

"I learned that God loves us. He really does. I don't know why, but He does. He doesn't want to lose one soul. He wants to bring us all back to live with Him for eternity."

"Even robbers, killers, the bully that tormented my son? Even me?" I asked.

"Well, that's one of the hardest parts to believe, especially you, but the answer's yes. It says in second Peter three, verse nine, that God 'does not want anyone to be destroyed but wants everyone to repent.' See? I know a little Bible stuff. Very little, but I'm learning it.

"They said that the Bible has the answers. But they also said that we cannot know everything about God's ways. The pastor said he had no better chance at getting to heaven than any of us did. Wow! I'd always thought that pastors and priests had a 'get into heaven free' card. This was some new way of thinking. I figured he'd say something like, 'If you can be as smart and important as me, then you'll get to heaven.' But he didn't. *Maybe he's not so smart,* I thought.

"I wasn't really sure about him at first. He didn't even have a priest uniform on. I thought that maybe he couldn't afford it, his clothes weren't fancy or expensive, just plain. And he didn't act pompous. I wondered how a regular-looking guy could know much about God. But he had a lot of good things to say, so I thought I'd come back a few times and see if his message was what I thought I heard.

"He said that rituals, though important, weren't as important as getting into an actual relationship with God. At that church, I learned that prayers come from your heart. I learned that God sent His only Son to save us because He loved us. I learned you only needed to believe to be saved. I learned that we could all be saints. And I learned that we don't pray to saints and don't call upon the angels to help us. We only can ask God to send them to help us. Only pray to the one true God the Father, the Son, and the Holy Spirit, three Persons in one God.

"That's a big one to figure, but it's a God thing—and I can't think as big as He can. My mind is the size of a flea's brain compared to His.

"But ya can't just sit back, put your boots on the highway pegs, and play easy rider, either! I was learning that it was more important to be in a relationship with God than to follow memorized rituals and prayers. This last part was hard to understand. I was always taught that with so many prayers or so many sacrifices or with bigger donations, you could earn your way to heaven. I made so many sets of First Friday Masses and litanies to the saints that I assumed I'd automatically get to heaven, so I was planning on coasting the rest of the way through life.

"I thought I'd earn my way to heaven, you know, be my own redeemer. The things I was about to learn would make me understand that the only way I could change was with the help of God. I couldn't do it on my own.

"It's like when husbands and wives argue without having God in their marriage, then the one who is the fanciest dancer with words wins.

Or, in my dad's case, the one who yelled the loudest. Without God in your marriage, you have no referee, you have nothing. You are nothing. So, it's easy to get tromped on or tromp on someone else. I learned that I had value, not because of any monetary gain but simply because God made me.

"But then to put all this into practice was going to be a big job. To believe that there was a God who really knew and loved me after all the bad things I'd done was a real challenge. That was going to take some hard thinking. The thing is that this whole idea seemed too easy to follow. Could it have been that simple? I wondered about that.

"This plainclothes pastor spoke with the authority of the Bible. And he said it all in words I could understand. Soon, it didn't matter that he didn't wear a fancy uniform. The words he spoke were truthful. They made sense to me. So, I thought I'd stick with that church and see what happened."

New Twins, 2004

"Time marched on, and my oldest, Young Charlie, got married. He was the one who'd had cancer and been hit by the train. He found a wonderful woman who truly loved him. He wanted children so much. But it wouldn't be easy with his history of chemotherapy. Young Charlie came to church with Charlie and me a couple of times. The pastor prayed over him and begged Jesus to touch him and his wife with a child.

"Miraculously, after a couple of years, they had twins, tiny gems, Olivia Ann and Helena Rae. I was fortunate enough to be able to keep the twins with me for a few days after they were born. The new mom and dad appreciated a good night's sleep. But I wasn't aware of how hard it was to watch twins, especially newborns. After a couple of days, even though Charlie helped me with the midnight feedings, I could hardly keep my eyes open.

"One night, I laid the babies down in a basket beside my bed and said a prayer for Jesus to keep them safe. They were not fully asleep, and I was worried that they would roll over each other. Still, I just couldn't keep my eyes open. I prayed and prayed, but my eyes closed.

"A couple of minutes later, I was awakened by light filtering through my eyelids. I opened my eyes. There around the basket was a whole bunch of angels in sherbet-colored gowns. They stood close around the basket like sardines, just like they were when I saw them over the golf course. I couldn't tell how many there were. But the twins were looking up at them and smiling. One angel turned and looked at me as if to say, 'Don't worry.' I knew the twins would be okay, so I fell back asleep."

"Is this true, too?" I asked.

"There you go again."

"No, I'm not ... I ... I'm sorry."

"When I woke up, the twins were sleeping, but that time, it seemed they had little smiles on their faces.

"My dad didn't come to see the twins at the Christening, because, he said, he'd had enough of babies.

"I liked to keep in touch with my sisters and brothers, but it always seemed that at least one of us was alienated from the others. We all generally got along okay on a very shallow level, but my dad continued to spin more stories about each of us. He drove us away from each other so much that I was always second-guessing the others' intents and motives. I figured I knew what they were thinking and that they were all laughing at me and criticizing the things I did, especially when I lost all that money on that get-rich-quick scheme. I thought we'd never be close again because of so much resentment, so much arguing.

"My dad wouldn't allow any of us in his house. He told people that we came into his house and stole things. He told me that my sisters had come over and had 'cleaned him out' of antiques and Mom's old jewelry and stuff. He was so constant with his criticism that I don't know why anyone ever took it seriously. The saying was that he was just Dad and that was the way he'd always been. But I thought he really must have meant what he was saying. I'd learned in church that what comes out of your mouth is drawn from the wellspring of your heart.

"One day, some of my sisters decided to surprise Dad for his birthday. He still had the old phonograph from the fifties. Some of our old records were still at his house because he'd kept them.

"I didn't want to go because he had already said so many lies about me. I couldn't even face my sisters or brothers. But they brought a cake and pizza and played old records and just visited. They were all happy to hear their old records. Everyone was visiting and having fun. It was only my dad and his children—most of them, anyway—and their spouses.

"The next morning, Dad called my sister Martha, yelling that she'd stolen the diamonds out of his phonograph needles in order to cash them in. He said he knew he'd had more needles and he remembered that she and her husband had been hiding in the corner, pretending to play records. Really, he said, they had been stealing the diamonds out of the phonograph needles. He called everyone to say we weren't allowed in his house again. Boy, was I glad I hadn't gone to that party.

"Many times, my sisters and brothers went over to take Dad food and presents on special days. He'd allow only one at a time in his house so he could keep watch and make sure that no one stole anything.

"He continued to tell each of us lies about the others. He told me that my brother Erik was trying to take all the old records that had my name on them. He told me that he had loaned my other brother, Jack, over twenty grand and that Jack never paid it back. He told my sisters that my husband was trapping squirrels and letting them loose in his house just to drive him mad. He told me that Sadie's husband asked him for a loan of one hundred and fifty thousand dollars.

"Dad was always knocking us down. I thought for sure that he must have had a mental illness or some emotional problems that had never been addressed. One time, I asked his sisters if he'd ever been abused or if something terrible had happened to him when he was a kid. My aunties said that their family life had been pretty normal and that my dad's younger brother turned out to be a really kind person. My dad was the only one who was like that in the family. I guess it was really true: 'It's just the way he is.'

"But I couldn't imagine someone believing his own outrageous lies and hating everyone so much. Even though Dad wasn't drinking all that much anymore, he was relentless on his hate campaign. I really thought he needed to see some kind of head doctor. But I didn't say any more about it, since I didn't want to cause any trouble.

"Charlie and I were still concerned about him, though. I guess we were like the rest and couldn't imagine that anyone could be so mean. We thought that in time he'd mellow out and be a loving guy filled with the wisdom of life.

"At that time we all had children of our own, and we just couldn't imagine anyone not loving their kids."

Dad&s Change of Heart, 2006

"All of a sudden, one day, my dad called and was really nice to me. He asked if Charlie would repipe his house and remodel his bathroom. The bathroom was old, and everything needed replacing. The piping in his house was rusted. He said he wanted to live there the rest of his life and needed to update some things so he'd be comfortable.

"I was elated. It seemed like my dad had changed his ways. It seemed that our prayers had a positive result. This was the dad I had always hoped was a good guy at heart. He said he trusted Charlie and me to be completely alone in the house. He told us that he didn't have a lot of money to spend, so I told him we'd charge him only for materials, no labor. He was very happy.

"He gave us the key and went on a cruise with his girlfriend, Millie. We repiped the house and tore out the old bathroom. We ran new copper pipe, re-tiled the bathroom, and put in new fixtures, countertops, and wall-to-wall mirrors. We put in a whirlpool tub in the bathroom as well as a new sink and faucet in the kitchen. We also put in a new kitchen floor. While Charlie was doing all that, I was cleaning the house. My dad promised to pay for the fixtures in the bathroom. He didn't pay for any of the labor or any of the kitchen items. He said he couldn't pay us for a couple months. But we were okay with that. We said a prayer to bless the house when Dad got home, and he seemed completely satisfied with the work. Then, a couple of weeks later, he wanted his sink rodded out. I went with Charlie and sat at the kitchen table, talking with Dad. As Charlie was finishing the job, he began cleaning up the floor and washing down the area under the sink. My dad began to make fun of him, asking me if I married a woman or what. He laughed because Charlie was scrubbing his floor 'like a woman'. Charlie heard that and told my dad that he always cleaned up like that on jobs. 'Yeah, well, you shoulda been a woman. You're sure acting like one,' Dad told him. Charlie was offended but didn't say anything.

"A couple of months after that, Dad didn't want to talk to us. I couldn't figure out why. When I called him, he would say that he was busy or that he didn't want to talk to me anymore. He would not give me a reason, just saying, 'You know.' I asked my sisters and brothers about it, but they said they didn't know anything. I guess they didn't want to start any trouble. Almost a year later, I found out that my dad had told my sisters and brothers that Charlie and I had searched his house and took out all his papers to see how much money he had. He said that we went through all his phonograph records, stole some, and ruined his phonograph. He said that Charlie put a new faucet in his kitchen so he could steal Dad's old faucet because it was more valuable and Charlie would resell it. I confronted Dad with these accusations. It was a year after we'd done the work; no one had told me about it until then. Dad said he'd never said that.

"It looked like the old dad was back. What fools my husband and I had been! Dad told me one story about my sisters and her children breaking into his house. He said that he had an ADT security system installed but that since my sister's husband was an electrician, he knew how to circumvent the system. I told him that that was impossible, but then he accused me of being in cahoots with them to rob his house.

"One day, I was on the phone with Dad. He had forgotten to turn his alarm off when he came into the house. The police came to the door to check on him. Dad set the phone down and forgot I was still on the line.

"I heard him tell the police that Martha's kids were coming into his house all the time and taking whatever they wanted. He said they take his food; they take his clothes and look for money. He said that because Martha lived across the street, she would know whenever he wasn't home and let them break in. I heard him tell the officer at the door that the police had caught the kids red-handed more than a few times but that he'd declined to press charges because they threatened to 'get even' with him. I was so mad because I knew it wasn't true.

"Martha had six kids, but they weren't 'kids'. Some were teachers, one was a doctor, and one was an internationally known glass artist. All of them were over thirty years old and had their own homes. Some had children of their own. They were the kind of 'kids' who'd find a dime on the floor, pick it up, and give you a quarter. Those 'kids' were angels.

"My dad had the officer believing him. I was so mad when I heard the officer say, 'Well, some people just don't know how to raise kids. She raised them to be lazy and they have no morals. They're just looking for free money.' I was yelling for the policeman to pick up the phone, but no one noticed that it was off the hook.

"My dad was like that, just telling lies about all his kids to whoever would listen. These were terrible lies! I was mad and called him back the next day. He told me that he couldn't wait to see every one of his kids in a casket. He said he prayed that at least some of our kids would wind up in a casket before he did. He said he didn't care if all of us went together or if we went one at a time. Our deaths were the only thing that would make him happy. He said that over and over.

"He cursed us and said that his prayers would be answered when he saw us all suffer the same as we made him suffer all those years. He said that he prayed every day that at least one of us would fall and become crippled for life.

"It was too hard for me to believe that he was just saying these things and not really meaning them. I had learned that what comes out of your mouth is from your heart. How could there be any exceptions to that rule?

"I don't know why, but my siblings and I still felt that Dad would be there if we needed him. After all, he was our father. We all felt sorry for him and still didn't stop calling him on the phone or refusing his calls. We still invited him over and bought him trips and other things. All of us pretty much accepted the fact that he didn't buy us any gifts for Christmas or birthdays. He told us that he'd spent enough on us when we were kids.

"My son Justin was visiting us one Christmas. Charlie and I asked my dad if Justin and Sarah could come over to visit him. My dad said that he didn't want to see them. If they came over, he wouldn't answer the door. He said he'd had enough grief from all of us. He accused them of looking for a handout.

"I remembered Christmases past and recalled how Dad would fight because he had to buy us gifts. He never bought us gifts when we were adults. Mostly, if he was going to come over, he'd bring a bottle of wine or whiskey. He never bought anything for the grandkids. He said that he had so many that he didn't even know their names. More than that, he said that he'd go broke if he had to buy them all presents.

"And he didn't want us to send him invitations to birthday parties. He said that people who sent announcements and invitations were just looking for donations from him and he wasn't giving any out.

"He didn't visit any of us on holidays, either, especially Christmas. He said we'd caused him enough trouble at Christmas when we were kids and that he didn't want to be reminded of it all.

"But I was trying to make all that I learned from church a part of my life. I wanted to see my dad as God could see him. And I wanted to help. He always was complaining that he was hurting. I figured that if he stopped hurting, then maybe he'd become a better person.

"One time, my dad said that his knees were hurting him really bad. My cousin was an orthopedic surgeon. He'd been on the cover of a medical magazine and had received awards acknowledging his work. He replaced knees for my husband and probably a thousand others. So, Charlie and I asked Dad if he wanted to go to my cousin and see if he could help him. My dad readily agreed.

"He said that it was actually our fault that his knees hurt. Driving a truck all those years, he had to hold his knees near the steering wheel, and that was the cause of his pain—all because he had to make money for the family. Everything was always our fault!

"My husband took my dad to the doctor's office. The doctor said that Dad had water on the knees. He removed the water and gave him a shot of something that cushioned the knees. The doctor told him that it wasn't a lifetime fix and that he'd need to come back from time to time. He didn't charge him anything, either. I don't know exactly what the procedure was, but I'd had it done to my knees and it really helped.

"Well, the next day, my dad called to say he was really feeling better. He thanked us. It looked like the old dad was mellowing out and maybe that our prayers for him were bearing fruit.

"And then, a few months later, my dad told everyone that Charlie and I had plotted with Doctor Michael to cripple him. He said that he had no idea what had been done to his knees, but he was having problems again. I told him he needed another treatment. I reminded him of what the doctor had told him. He said he never knew what was going on in the doctor's office.

"He said that Charlie had asked him to go with because Charlie had to see the doctor and was afraid to go alone. So Dad said that he'd gone with Charlie to keep him company. He claimed that he'd only wanted to ask Doctor Michael what he might recommend for treatment of his knees. I told Dad that that was absurd. Charlie had no problem going alone anywhere.

"But Dad told everyone that he saw Charlie and Doctor Michael hiding in the corner and laughing it up about how they were going to cripple my dad. He said that he'd heard them plotting. Then he said that all he remembered about the rest of the visit was while Charlie held Dad down, Doctor Michael gave him a shot and pulled all the water out of his knees so there'd be no more cushioning between his kneecap and bone and Dad heard him laugh and say 'that will cripple him up good'. I told Dad that wasn't what had happened at all, but he called me a liar.

"Dad called the medical board and the hospital where Doctor Michael practiced and threatened a lawsuit, calling my cousin a butcher. He kept calling the doctor's office and threatening Michael. Then, he'd tie up the phone lines by calling the office and hanging up. His calls were so constant and threatening that I told Dad that if he made one more call to the office, I'd tell the receptionist to call the police on him. I cannot believe that my cousin didn't sue him for slander.

"I didn't want to be around my dad. With my new beliefs and understanding, I wanted to tell him I thought he was losing his mind. I wanted him to go to a psychiatrist. But the rest of my family didn't think that he was any different than he'd been his whole life and actually they were right. They suggested I not say anything and not cause any trouble;

otherwise, it would look like I was after his money. They said he didn't really mean the bad things he said. And even my aunties said, 'If you want to be a good Christian you must honor your father. Turn the other cheek.' But listening to his diatribe against all of us was making me very angry and too stressed out to think of anything else.

"His abuse was not confined to his children. He hated his grandchildren with the same passion. He seemed to really zero in on Martha's sons and daughters. One of her sons, the internationally known glass artist, had his works displayed in the museum of art in Michigan. Martha was very proud of that. When we told my dad about this, he just laughed. He said that the museum was probably a combination gas station, grocery store, fruit stand, and museum. He said that he saw lots of those kinds of museums during the old days when he was on the road to Minnesota in the fifties. He said, 'The kid's a dummy,' he said Martha's son was lying to everyone by saying that his stuff was in a real museum. But I knew that wasn't true. Her son was really talented, and his work was indeed featured in an art museum.

"One time, Dad said that Martha's other son was sneaking into his house with his girlfriend and turning his thermostat up all the way so the furnace would burn out.

"Dad had a player piano that had been in the family for quite a while. It needed a little repair. Several of us asked if we could have it so we could fix it up. He told all of us that he'd chop it up and throw it in the alley before he'd give it to any of us. And he did. When he no longer wanted it, he and his girlfriend, Millie, sawed it up into small pieces and threw it away.

"Then there was an old roaster stand that had been in the basement for years. My mom used to put her roaster on it every Thanksgiving. The roaster was gone, but the stand was still there, old and rusty. Helen wanted it for sentimental reasons. But Dad said that Millie had told him that it was junk. She had thrown it in the alley."

"Why are you telling me all this stuff? Why are you telling me how dumb you were to keep going back for more?" I asked.

"I guess I have to tell you so that you or I can sort it out, so that you can figure out the whys of who I am. But it's mainly so you can understand the situation and find the answers you need so desperately.

"After not talking to him for months, Dad called me one day as if nothing had happened. One more chance, I thought."

"Oh, you fool! You totally brainwashed idiot!"

"On that, you're right! He talked about the old times when we used to go on trips together to the lake. So, Charlie and I thought that maybe this time he'd really changed. We thought that God was testing us and we shouldn't turn our backs on my dad. After all, he was getting older—and maybe, just maybe, he could change. We decided to take him on a trip like we did years ago. We wanted to make things really special and as much fun as possible for him. We decided to rent a little cabin on the water.

"On the way out there he said, 'Don't get any ideas that I'm gonna buy you a place on the lake.' I asked him why he thought that. He said, 'One of your sisters or maybe one of your brothers told me that's why you asked me to go on this trip.' I asked him who had said that, and he just shrugged it off and said, 'I don't want to get anyone in trouble. I should have just kept my mouth shut.' I dropped the subject, but I made a note to find out who had said such a thing to him. Later I found out no one said that.

"Several times on the trip, he told me he wanted to talk about his money. He said he wanted someone to help him take charge, wanting to make sure that some of us got nothing. He asked me what I thought of each one of my brothers and sisters and what I would recommend he leave each one. He said some terrible things about all of them. And then he said that he wanted to make me executor of his estate if I would do what he asked and make sure that some of my siblings got nothing.

"I told him he'd have to figure that out himself. If he left anything, I said, if he even had anything to leave, then it should be equally distributed among his children.

"That kind of talk made me very uncomfortable, because he'd said the same to my sisters and brothers. To one of us, he'd brag about how much money he had, and then he'd tell the others that that one was trying to find out how much he had so they could be his executor and take it all.

"So, I just kept changing the subject. He got angry and told me that

I was taking sides against him. He promised that if I wouldn't help, then he'd find the meanest person he could to do what he wanted. Then, he'd cut me out. I just rolled my eyes.

"That conversation ended quickly when Charlie came into the room with a good idea. Since my father had problems walking, Charlie offered to rent a wheelchair and take him along the docks to see all the boats to enjoy the scenery. Dad was almost hysterical when refusing to do that. He sat in the house most of the time. Later, we learned that he'd told everyone that we wanted to get him a wheelchair so we could push him off the dock into the water so he would drown and we could get his money.

"He'd complain that he couldn't sleep, but on the second night at the cabin, he said he'd slept well. Later, he told my brothers and sisters that Charlie and I slipped something into his food to put him to sleep. He told them that he wouldn't come over again and eat or drink anything at our house because he thought we were trying to poison him. He also told them that we left him alone the whole time to go bar-hopping with our friends, which was another lie.

"On our way home from the trip, we came to a town that was having a festival. There were stage shows in the street and booths with food, art, and crafts. We asked my dad if he wanted to stop, and he said yes.

"We got him a chair in front to watch the stage show. Then, Charlie and I walked around to look at the crafts. When we went back to get my dad, he was talking to a gentleman he had just met. Apparently, the man had something to do with sponsoring the kids who were in the show.

"I overheard my dad asking the man for his name and address. My dad told him that he'd like to send him some money because he loved to help kids like these who were trying to make something of themselves; kids who worked for what they wanted.

"Then he started talking about his kids, who just wanted to steal from him. 'They don't want to work or make a dime on their own. They're too lazy. They want it all handed to them. They're all just waiting for me to die so they can get my money.' I heard him vow to the man that his kids wouldn't get a dime.

"Oh, God, nothing had changed with him. All everyone did was for nothing. It was a true waste of time."

"And what was the matter with you? You kept doing the same thing, wasting time on him. Fool! There's a difference between being respectful and being a punching bag. I don't even feel sorry for you anymore!" I said.

"Where have you been all my life? Why didn't you come to me sooner? I would have listened. I know I would have listened. If only I'd known."

The young woman started crying. I could feel the pain she was experiencing.

"He told us over and over that he wished we were all dead," she said. "'When each one of you is in a box in the ground, then I'll be happy,' he'd say. I can't even count how many thousands of time he said that.

"He began to accuse my brother Jack of having an affair with his girlfriend, Millie. One time, my brother planned to visit Dad for his birthday. Jack's plane was late, and he stopped to pick up pizza. By the time he got to Dad's, Dad was fuming. He accused Jack of being late because he'd been sleeping with Dad's girlfriend. He threw the food at Jack and told him to get out. He raised his cane as if to hit Jack, and then he told Jack to go ahead and try to hit him so he could call the police and have him locked up. But Jack never tried to hit him. Jack left broken-hearted and beaten up, which was usual when he was with Dad.

"Soon after that, my dad began accusing Helen's husband of having an affair with Millie. He started calling my brother-in-law 'lover boy.'

"When we tried to stay away from him, Dad would call one or two of us and get sympathy after saying he was lonely. Then, that person would really go out of the way to help him again, figuring that Dad had changed.

"Helen sent her cleaning lady, a woman she had known for twenty years, over to clean his house. Helen paid her to do the cleaning. Dad seemed to appreciate that. But a week or so later, he called all of us to tell us that Theresa had been stealing his shirts to sell at the flea market. He called Theresa several times on the phone, calling her a wetback and saying that that he was going to have her arrested. He left terrible, threatening messages on her phone. She recorded them, and I heard them. I told her that she should take that to the police. Dad's message said that her whole family was here illegally and he'd get them deported. That was not true. I urged Theresa to sign a complaint against my dad, but she decided not to say anything. She didn't want to cause Helen or him any trouble.

"A few months after that, Martha talked our dad into going to dinner with all his sons and daughters, who were all in town at the same time. I didn't know that he was going to be there. I thought I was just going to meet with my sisters and brothers. Helen didn't tell me until we were almost at the restaurant. I wouldn't have gone if I had known that my dad was going to be there. I wanted to stay away from him. As soon as Helen and I walked in, Dad told the others he hadn't been expecting to see us. He said he hoped he would never have had to see us again.

"He started telling Helen how she sent Theresa to steal things out of his house. Helen moved to the other end of the table so as not to start anything. Then, Dad started making fun of some of us, saying that we were looking pretty old and wrinkled. He then zoomed in on Jack, telling him how stupid he was, saying he didn't even know what state he lived in.

"Things got so bad that I went to the bathroom to secretly say a prayer, asking God to tell me what to do. I came back and said, 'Dad, this hate stuff has got to stop.' He got up, tried to hit me with his cane, and yelled real loud, saying, 'Death is coming to you, girl. I wish you death, death to you and your family, you Satan, you Devil. Stay away from me.' And he added in some swearwords, right there in the restaurant, which he yelled out really loud. I could hardly believe it. Everyone was looking at us as he tried to clobber me with his cane."

"Oh no, do you think he cursed your son that way?" I asked.

"No. I know now that God doesn't work like that. God doesn't listen to prayers of hate. If He did, then the world would have been devoid of people long ago. But just to know that my dad said that to me out loud in a restaurant, wishing death to my whole family, was just too much for me. I really tried to keep away from him after that.

"But I heard he still was filled with rage for me. I heard that one day my dad was sitting on his porch and saw a landscaping guy, about eighteen or twenty years old, who was cutting the neighbor's grass. He called the guy over and asked him if he would cut his grass. Prior to that, Martha's kids always cut his grass, raked his leaves, and shoveled his snow. He never paid them, and they never asked to be paid. They were just doing those things to help him out.

"See? This is what I didn't understand. Everyone had always been so good to him throughout all the years, and everyone had been so hurt by him. How long did we have to continue being beaten up? But if we stood up to him, were we sinning by not honoring our father? Were we the bad people? Would we be taking a chance on losing his love for us if we stood up to him?"

"I see what your questions are, but I don't think that God would want you all to be so beat up all the time. And I'm not so sure that you'd be losing something that was clearly never there," I said.

"Yeah, well, anyway, back to the grass cutting. The guy, Angelo, came over and cut Dad's grass, and then Dad brought out a couple of beers and sat talking with him. Then, Dad brought him into the house, where they stayed several hours.

"Martha lived across the street. She got a little worried. Dad hadn't known this Angelo before that day. So, she called Dad. Angelo answered. When Martha asked to talk to Dad, Angelo yelled, 'Hey, she's yelling at me, just like you said!'

"So my dad grabbed the phone and told Martha to leave Angelo alone, that she was just jealous. Angelo was a good kid and that he wished he'd had at least one good kid like him he could be proud of. My dad said that he was going to have Angelo do some extensive remodeling for him and give him a lot of money. Then, he hung up.

"Next thing, Martha saw Angelo driving my dad's car away. It was unclear if my dad was in the car or not. She was thinking that maybe Angelo robbed my dad and stole his car. So, she called Dad again but got no answer. She called me and asked if I'd heard from him. I hadn't. I was concerned, so I called the police for a well-being check, because no one really knew this Angelo. We thought that maybe Dad needed help, especially after Martha saw Angelo squeal away in our dad's car.

"Martha and her husband went over to Dad's to see if he was alright. My dad came out, screaming for them to get off his porch. He said he had a gun and couldn't wait to shoot them in the head. He said that he'd love to see Martha's husband bleeding to death on the sidewalk and that he knew he'd get away with it because he'd say he was just an old man and he was scared. He'd say they were trying to break in again and he'd had to stop them. He told Martha that he hoped her daughter would get hit by a bus. He said he gave Angelo the car to use for whatever he wanted.

"When the police showed up, Martha didn't want to get my dad in trouble for the gun so she didn't say anything. She told the police that he was okay and there'd been a misunderstanding.

"That kind of thing continued for years. So many more incidents like that! It was one of us at a time. He'd go after one or two of us, not talking to us for months, and then he would call as though nothing ever happened.

"I guess we always thought that was just how he was."

Selling the Big House, 2013

"Dad's house was always kept as it was, suspended in time. Dad wouldn't let any one of us in. We thought as he was getting older, he might want to move to one of those retirement villages. We didn't think he should live alone, and he didn't want any of us in his house to help him with anything, because, according to him, we were just looking for his money.

"But he did fall a couple of times, and each time he'd call one of us to help him. It was hard for him to get around, but he didn't want any of us in his house to help him. Also, he didn't want to have any caregivers come in because they would try to rob him blind.

"Each of us offered him accommodations in our homes and even said that he could have his own space in each of our houses and take turns visiting with us. I can't believe I offered, too! He said that he didn't want to live with any of us and that he was thinking of selling his house, thinking that he could make a lot of money on it.

"Helen's husband and Sadie were realtors. My dad was seriously considering selling his house and then moving into a retirement home. He asked them to find out what his house was worth. They told him the price he could get.

"A couple of his grandkids made him offers on the house, good offers, three hundred and seventy-five thousand dollars. He told them that he'd never sell it for less than three hundred and ninety-five thousand dollars and that if he couldn't get that, then he wouldn't leave the house he'd lived in for over sixty years. So, we let things be. We didn't suggest that he move anymore.

"But he loved to call different realtors and ask what they would sell the house for. He loved to tell them how money-hungry all his kids were. He'd tell them terrible things about us.

"One day, I saw an Andy's Realty for-sale sign in front of Dad's house. I called Andy, the realtor, and tried to explain to him about my dad. He said, 'Your dad told me you'd all be calling me and complaining. He told me how money-hungry you all are, and he said you'd try to make trouble. Your dad is lonely, and none of you ever even visit him unless you want more of his money.'

"I told him that Dad had never given us any money. I told him that Dad was ninety-three and that he had seven kids, over twenty grandkids, three living sisters, and one living brother, not to mention his great-grandchildren. Andy told me to mind my own business. I asked him if he'd talked to any one of my sisters or brothers before my dad signed the contract. He said he did, but when I talked with my brothers and sisters, they said they did not talk to Andy. They found out only after Dad had signed. It looked like my dad had met a suave realtor who'd convinced him to sell his house.

"According to my Dad and Andy, he took Dad to the store and to the bank as many times as Dad asked. He helped him write his checks and he'd visit with my dad and tell him that he'd be with him to the end, doing whatever my dad wanted. He told my dad that he should sell the house as is, with everything in it. He said that nothing in it was worth anything and that Dad would have to pay to get any of the old stuff hauled away. My dad told Andy to take whatever he wanted for himself. And Andy did. He had the keys and helped himself to anything he wanted.

"In one week, the house sold for two hundred and eight-four thousand dollars. My dad netted only two hundred and sixty-four thousand. What a fool he was. Any one of his grandkids would have paid more than that.

"Wednesday before the closing, Dad called Janet, the youngest, and asked her to help him move. He told her that she could take some things, but not to give anything to any of the others. He warned her not to tell anyone, either!

"He called my brother Jack and ordered him to take out the big television set and chop it up on the front lawn to show everyone that he'd sooner destroy it than let any of his kids have something that had belonged to him. He especially wanted Martha to see that she'd get nothing from him. Jack refused to do that.

"Though I didn't know it then, Janet had a secret plan to save what she could and secretly share it with the rest of us. Friday, two days before the closing, my dad called me and said he'd sold the house and that we could take anything that was left after Andy had taken what he wanted. He told me that he let Janet and Jack into the house on Wednesday and that they pretty much cleaned him out of everything. He insisted that he hadn't wanted it that way. He said that he'd wanted all of us to have something but that those two had just 'cleaned him out' of all the stuff that was worth anything.

"Too late, though. The closing was on a Sunday night. My dad didn't use the attorney he'd always used in the past. Andy provided an attorney for him.

"At first, I wasn't going to go to the house, but Helen said that we should at least go together to look. Then, I figured that it was my home, too, and this would be my last chance to see it. One last visit might be good.

"We had to wait for Andy to give us the key. He said that he had to get some things out on Saturday and wouldn't let us in until Sunday at noon. The new people were to come in on Monday at noon.

"I went with Helen to the house, and we were aghast at what we saw—tax returns, medical records, a few old pictures, Dad's passport, old bank accounts, new bank account statements, and lots of paperwork scattered all over the table. The closets were filled with clothes, and the fridge was still filled with food. Shoes and underwear were strewn about.

"I was angry because all the stuff my dad had been hoarding, all his financial information, the greeting cards we had sent my mother for birthdays, and Social Security cards, had been left out for anyone to see. All this time, not allowing any of us into the house, he was saving everything ... for what?

"Helen and I went straightaway to look for the big box of old pictures.

It was really the only thing we would have wanted. It was a big box about three feet high, just filled with old black-and-white photos of us as kids and of my mom and dad when they got married. I remember there were photos of us with Santa, photos of us at Kings Park View, and photos of relatives we hadn't seen for a long time. But Helen and I found no box of pictures in Dad's house. He probably threw it out, or maybe Andy took it. We felt really bad that it was gone. It would have been nice to show our kids pictures of us when we were little. Our hearts were heavy.

"You should have expected that. When did you think he might have magically started caring about any of you? Why did you even go?" I asked.

"I would have left it all and walked away, but my son Justin had asked me to get him some remembrance of my mom, maybe a Christmas ornament or something like that. But I couldn't go through everything that day. I was worried that my dad's personal information would be stolen. I shouldn't have even cared! I just wanted to get whatever memorabilia I could that would have meant something to each of my brothers and sisters. I hustled to get out as many things as possible in three hours on Monday morning. But I found that most of it was just junk.

"When I got home, I wrote an incredibly mean e-mail to Janet and Jack and shared my judgment call with the rest of my family. You see, I'd believed what my dad had said they'd done. I accused Janet and Jack of all sorts of things. I called them pigs at the trough. I called her Dorian Gray. I don't even want to remember the rest! I told them that I had thought we were all a family but that I could see they were greedy like Dad.

"I fell into one of Dad's schemes to get us all arguing. I can't believe I was so stupid. And I so regret the things I wrote! But I couldn't call it back. No, you can't retrace your steps and pull back the hurt you caused!"

"I know that all too well!" I said.

"What a fool I'd been. That was the one time in my life when I really should have not said anything!"

"When did you ever learn? You were really as mean and stupid as—"

"Watch it! I never said the rules changed. Shut up and listen!"

"Sorry."

"I had all the stuff moved to my and Charlie's garage, and I began to go through the things. There were none of the old Christmas ornaments I remembered, none of the many decorations that Mom loved so much. There was not one of her little Dresden figurines or the little Christmas skaters. Plus, the train set was gone. There was none of her costume jewelry or even her old jewelry box. But I did find many terrible notes that my dad had written. They were in desk and dresser drawers. 'You palooka, hands off!' 'No money here for you.' 'Get your rotten thieving hands out of here.' 'Drop dead if you touch anything here.'

"It felt like I was holding something evil and disgusting in my hands. I quickly put the notes on the side to show Helen. I found some old pornography books. I threw those out right away. I found unopened Christmas cards I'd sent to Dad. I found a few of the old 45s I'd bought when I was in my teens, as well as a few that my sisters had bought. But all our treasured ones were gone: The Kingston Trio, The Beatles, Elvis, and so many more, all the original ones we bought as kids. All the remaining records had stickers with 'Dad's' written on them.

"I found my mom's death certificate, high school diploma, and autopsy report. How sad we felt. I found a few of my brothers' and sisters' pictures, pictures from our graduations and First Communions crumpled up, left for garbage.

"The hurt was so deep that no one wanted anything that was left. We saved some pictures and cards. We gave the furniture to Goodwill.

"There was an old moving dolly left in the house. My dad specifically asked my brother if he wanted it. Jack said that he'd let him know. Dad called my brother several times more times. So, Jack finally said yes. My dad said, 'Good! I'll make sure you never get it.' He took it with him and stuck it in his room at the retirement community just to make sure that Jack would never get it. It's there today, sitting in the middle of his room, taking up space, being used for nothing. But he wanted to be sure that Jack knew he had it and wouldn't give it to him.

"Dad told people at his retirement place that we were all asking for money. Sometimes, he told them that he was giving us money, lots. But he wasn't. He told them all we live in nice houses and that we made all our money off his back. Then he told them that we took his house away and stuck him in a home.

"I know now that none of us ever meant anything to him, not even my mom. If he did even care about her, he wouldn't have left her personal papers out for everyone to see. I knew it. This time, I really knew it. He meant everything he said about us. He really did hate us. All the years came flooding back, all the beatings, the abuse, the mean things he'd done to my family. I never realized how much my poor mother suffered living with him. Maybe it was good that God took her early. She deserved better than what she had with him on this earth.

"Money was all-important to my dad. But I realize now that he got all his money by denying his wife and his kids everything and then charging us for everything he could. No one else I know ever had to pay their father 'room and board' at the age of fourteen. He accused us of stealing from him, but in reality, he was stealing from us. I realize now that I wasted much of my life believing that I was worthless. I wasted much of my time trying to make my dad like me when I should have been an adult caring for my own family.

"But I didn't know it then, when I was younger. All I knew was that he was my dad, like our loving Father, God our protector. I thought that our dad always cared about us and loved us. I considered what Jesus said in chapter seven of Matthew, in verses nine and ten: 'Which of you, if his son asks for bread, will give him a stone? Or if he asked for a fish, will give him a scorpion?' I'll tell you which one—my dad. My dad would give us stone. My dad would give us a scorpion, but not even that if he could sell it for cash.

"That house, the way it was sold the things he gave to strangers, the pictures—none of it meant anything to him. It wasn't so much that he'd sold the house. It was the way he'd done it. He'd sold it for over a hundred thousand dollars less, just so his family wouldn't have it.

"I guess I always thought we'd all get together, you know, family ties, sticking together. None of us wanted to take anything that someone else wanted. Jack didn't, Janet didn't. No one did. We'd have all shared things, gone through some memories, put to rest some things that had been said about us. They were all good people.

"But that never happened. My mean accusations ensured that. Was I angry? Oh yes. But then, the anger I had for him left quickly. I turned it on myself. I hated myself.

"All of that was in the past. It took me too long to realize that my dad had robbed us all of what it meant to be a family. I realized I'd wasted all that time listening to lies, making up lies, and never seeking the truth.

"I goofed up on understanding the thing about 'honor thy father.' Instead, I was breaking you know, the most important, the first commandment, 'Have no other gods before me.' You know, don't worship golden idols? Well, I'd made my dad into a god and worshipped him before anything else. So, I guess you could say that I let him be my golden idol while I ignored the real God.

"That's the worst sin. Maybe that's why I have to pay such a high price."

The young woman was suddenly silent. The darkness was closing in around me. "Which way do I go now?" I asked. When she didn't answer, I turned and saw that she was gone. I didn't even know her name, but I think I really did. I yelled, "Hey! Where are you? Where do I go from here?" I was lost, stuck there. I started to cry.

I could hear the radio playing again off in the distance: "He's a devil, not a man, and he'll hurt you if he can …"

I began to understand things better. My tears flowed. I cried about the wasted time and my ignorance. I did it all on my own. I was responsible. I shed tears for time I lost with my family, so many tears of regret and guilt. I reached into my pocket for a tissue, and that's when I found the handle of the knife. It was still there.

"Now, you see that it always was your fault. All your life, you did nothing but cause trouble. You are bad, always were, time to come with me." It was the Devil's voice, and the voice was real. "You're mine and you belong to me now!" Maybe it's time, time for me to pay up.

No, start the bike now, move before it's too late. Follow the music.

I saw the owl, almost out of sight. I got on the bike and roared away from the voice. I was afraid and wanted to get out of there. It was too dark to see where I was going.

Follow the music.

The radio, I could hear it a little louder: "Can't you see that big green tree where the water's running free?"

Was I traveling back into the swamp or away from it? God help me, O Jesus, help me. Just then, the owl swooped down over me. I followed the owl slowly as it flew. I didn't want to make too much noise and scare it away. Just ahead, I saw the little girl. I got off the bike and ran to her. She looked so different. She was all cleaned up—no knots in her hair, no bites on her arms. Most of all, her fingers and toes showed no signs of blood. They were trimmed neatly, and not a cuticle was shredded. She almost had a glow about her.

"Do you forgive me for everything, for being bad?" she asked me.

"How could I not forgive you? There's nothing to forgive! Such an innocent, you never were bad, never!" I hugged her tightly, and my tears fell on her shirt. I was so remorseful for hating her all those years!

I heard a slight noise behind me. It was the young woman whom I first saw on the motorcycle. She looked really different, too. She was stunning, as if she'd just stepped out of a fashion magazine. Her brown hair had turned a little gray. Her clean complexion shone, and all the insect bites were healed. The bald patch on her head was filled in with shining hair, and her hands were manicured. She looked older, wiser, and less aggressive.

"And me? Do you forgive me?" she asked.

"For what, you've done nothing wrong, not to me. You've only hurt yourself by searching in the wrong places."

"I did. I know now that I couldn't find it with a foul, loud mouth and a bottle of, well, just a bottle of dope. I stopped drinking, you know. I've been talking to God pretty regularly. I'm near convinced that He likes me. And, you know, He's been here all along. I just couldn't see."

"But I can see now. He loves you. I know He does. And I do, too," I said.

The woman reached into one of her saddlebags, which seemed to be slowly fading. *Not another bottle,* I thought.

"Here. I brought you these flowers as some memories you may want to keep. No pictures left, just these blue tulips. There's not much else back there that's any good." She pointed back into the dark swamp. "They're the only ones I found; they're what you were looking for. They're the few good memories of our past, yours, mine, and hers. One of the good ones is Justin."

I hugged her. We both started crying. I turned to the little girl, picked her up, and smothered her with hugs and kisses.

"I have something for you, too," the little girl said.

I set her down, and she jumped into a hole under the tree to get something.

"Here. This is for you." She handed me her Jesus statue, the one she'd had all that time. "He kept me safe, and now He'll keep you safe. He was with us all the time. You know that now, don't you?" she asked.

"But it's yours. I can't take this," I said.

"Yes, you can. You'll need to know Him as I do. And, really, it's yours, anyway."

"Oh, thank you, thank you so much!" I held the statue to my heart and cried so hard that my eyes closed. I whispered a prayer: "O God, thank you, thank you."

When I opened my eyes, the girl was gone. I looked for the biker, but she was gone, too. This was the reality of my life: an innocent little girl, a lost woman. Oh no, I could never condemn them. But would God condemn us? Would He forgive us? They were never bad. None of us had been bad, lost, yes but never bad.

I am no longer that frightened little girl sitting on the steps biting her nails till her hands were bloody, shaking, not saying anything or starting any trouble. I was too busy trying to act like my dad, following in his footsteps, trying to make him like me.

The little girl was no longer a child but a distant memory.

The biker woman had been lost but was found when she let God pull her from the swamp.

Now, they are both just memories somehow saved from blackness. And I'm left here alone, alone and lost. *Why am I still here? What comes next?*

Is there still time? What does the final chapter hold?

The White Owl, 2014

The two are gone now, part of what was. But where did that leave me? I still couldn't see the way out of the swamp, and I had more things that needed to be answered. *Am I really forgiven?*

I closed my eyes and lifted my head to say a small prayer, hoping that I'd receive the peace of the Lord. I asked Him to comfort me in my grief and give me the understanding I needed to go on, if that's what He wanted. I asked if He would take me right then. I didn't know how to go on. I really didn't want to. I wanted to end it all. Too many mistakes made. *Maybe God can forgive me, but can I forgive me?*

I couldn't stop crying. My eyes had almost swollen shut. I was drowning in self-pity when I heard a branch crack. I opened my eyes and saw the white owl looking quizzically down at me. He paused and soared low, illuminating a path I hadn't noticed. I saw a ray of hope. Before I had a chance to think, I grabbed my Jesus statue and my bouquet of blue tulip memories.

I followed the white owl, walking as quickly as I could. It stopped and landed on a branch. It didn't seem to notice me as it preened its feathers. With darkness all around, I'd never find my way out alone. So, I sat down for a little while, waiting for the owl to make another move.

I was no longer the person I was. I would not let my past define me. *But I'm old, and it's too late,* I thought.

I started to cry again when I remembered that I'd never gotten the chance to give my son Justin anything I salvaged from the big old house. He'd have loved some of the old memories, but they were all gone, replaced with those evil notes my dad had written. I didn't want him to see those, anyway.

It was only a few weeks later that my boy was gone, gone to heaven.

I wanted to die. *Why won't my body just let me die? Then I could tell him in person.*

I looked back and remembered all the times Justin had spoken of his fears. I hadn't realized that they were real. I'd been too busy feeding pearls to swine. And those I'd misjudged were the first to appear at my side, offering help and comfort. I couldn't believe that they'd overlooked my mean e-mail and the wall I'd built up between us.

The first ones I called for help were my sisters and brothers. They took care of my plane tickets to California, took care of preparing the memorial service. They took care of everything.

These people, these people I called pigs and worse these people I was told had always been laughing at me and hating me. How sad it was that I'd misjudged them all those years and had taken great pride in insulting them whenever I could. Here they were, helping me, crying with me, feeling the great loss of my child.

Dad never showed any sense of loss for his grandson. He offered no condolences but only said that he really liked that kid and wanted to see him the past Christmas, but apparently Justin hadn't had time to visit his grandfather.

I reminded my dad that he hadn't wanted to see Justin when Charlie and I offered. He said that was only for that day, that he would have made time if we'd insisted. He didn't attend Justin's memorial service.

My dad lives in a retirement village now, still saying the same terrible things about all of us, still counting his pile of dollars, which is quickly dwindling, still tripping over the aluminum dolly he wanted to make sure Jack didn't get.

O the time I wasted! What did it matter if he ever cared?

Then I thought I heard a voice. "Those who love money will never have enough. How meaningless to think that wealth brings true happiness" (Ecclesiastes 5:10). But no one was there. Then, my mind was filled with answers. No one can change except with the help of God.

It's not a cliché to say that a person must be born again. It was my fault that I'd handed my life over to someone else who told me what to do and who to be. Sure, the falls and stumbles had gotten me to where I was at that point, but I'd done so much damage along the way.

Through knowing Jesus, I knew I wasn't worthless. I was His possession, but I honestly couldn't see what good He might see in me.

"God created you in his own image."

I looked at the owl. *Is it talking, or is it my imagination? This isn't Disneyland,* I told myself. But after all that had happened, a talking owl didn't surprise me.

"Is this what it's come to?" I asked. "Like Doctor Dolittle, I talk to the animals? Do you have the answers?"

"I do," the owl whispered. "Give all your worries and cares to God, for He cares about you" (1 Peter 5:7).

"You did talk to me, but how and why?" I asked.

It seemed that the owl knew my thoughts. *Has God been there all my years? Have I been so blind that I didn't see Him? How will we all get through this? What about Sarah? What does she have to look forward to? She's brokenhearted. And me, do I have any future? Right now, I don't know if I even want one!*

"The Lord isn't really being slow about His promise, as some people think. No, He is being patient for your sake" (2 Peter 3:9). "May he grant your heart's desires and make all your plans succeed" (Psalm 20:4). "'For I know the plans I have for you,' says the Lord. 'They are plans for good and not for disaster, to give you a future and a hope. In those days when you pray, I will listen. If you look for me wholeheartedly, you will find me'" (Jeremiah 29:11–13).

What about the bully, that ugly thing who taunted my Justin?

"God is an honest judge. He is angry with the wicked every day. If a person does not repent, God will sharpen his sword. He will bend and string his bow. He will prepare his deadly weapons and shoot his flaming arrows" (Psalm 7:11–13).

I'm so weak now.

"Turn and answer me, O Lord my God! Restore the sparkle to my eyes, or I will die!" (Psalm 13:3). I screamed.

What about those tiny embryos, the baby?

"You must serve only the Lord your God. If you do, I will bless you with food and water, and I will protect you from illness. There will be no miscarriages or infertility in your land, and I will give you long full lives" (Exodus 23:25–26).

My son Justin had been seeking God. He'd had so many questions. Was he wrong to doubt you, to ask and seek the answers?

"The Lord welcomes questions. He has all the answers."

Is there a God? Is there really a God?

"Only fools say in their hearts, 'There is no God.' They are corrupt, and their actions are evil; not one of them does good! The Lord looks down from heaven on the entire human race; he looks to see if anyone is truly wise, if anyone seeks God" (Psalm 14:1–2).

Justin had sought God to answer his questions.

"You belong to God, my dear children. You have already won a victory over those people because the Spirit who lives in you is greater than the spirit who lives in the world" (1 John 4:4).

I want to believe. I used to believe. I used to understand. I want to understand again. But God is beyond my understanding.

"Trust in the Lord with all your heart; do not depend on your own understanding. Seek His will in all you do, and he will show you which path to take" (Proverbs 5:6).

How do I forgive all the bad things that have been done to me, and to Justin and Sarah?

"Leave them to God! He has given you many good things."

"If you repay good with evil, evil will never leave your house" (Proverbs 17:13). "Walk with the wise and become wise; associate with fools and get into trouble" (Proverbs 13:19).

And my son, my boy. Is he with Jesus in heaven?

"And just as God raised Christ Jesus from the dead, He will give life to your mortal bodies by this same spirit living within you" (Romans 8:11). "I will not die; instead I will live to tell what the Lord has done" (Psalm 118:17).

The owl spread its wings as if to fly away, but it stayed in one spot. *Oh, don't go!*

The wings grew large, and suddenly the creature was no longer a snowy owl. It slowly morphed into a familiar shape as it moved closer to me. At once, I knew.

Yes, Mom. Justin's thoughts came to me. *I'm in heaven.*

Justin! O Justin! It's you! You're here! You're okay!

"The light shines in the darkness, and the darkness can never extinguish it" (John 1:5).

I'll see you soon. And please, tell everyone I love them all, Justin told me.

But are you … are you happy? Don't you miss us all?

Mom, it'll be only a short time before we'll all be together again. Here, it's like a minute. Mom, you wouldn't believe how beautiful this is. I think that if everyone knew how beautiful this is, they'd all want to leave earth as soon as possible. Maybe that's why you don't hear so much about heaven.

Oh, honey then you're happy? I mean, I—

I know what you mean, Mom. I'm happy, and all of you will see this too one day.

Baby, do you forgive me? Can you ever forgive me for neglecting you so much?

Mom, you never neglected me. You were just a child yourself. I always knew you loved me.

And Sarah, can you let her know how much you lo—

I'm letting her know, Mom. I see her always. I know her heart is broken and I never wanted that to happen. I love her then and I love her now. I'm always with her. When the baby arrives, she'll understand, and I'll be with them then, too.

I wish she were here. I wish you could stay, I, I— You know, I bought you a Star Wars original lunch box for Christmas, and a Disneyland one, too, and I even found an original vinyl Pinocchio record, but now, I, I won't see you to—

I saw it. I know. You spent so much on them! Mom, give it to our baby, mine and Sarah's.

Can't you stay? Can't you stay with us?

I am with you, Mom. I'm with all of you, all the time.

I held him for a long time, crying, wishing that I could stay with him. And then he was gone. I was happy, sad, and exhausted after all that had happened.

"I lay down and slept yet I woke up in safety for the Lord was watching over me" (Psalm 3:5).

My Boy

When I awoke I was no longer in the swamp. I understood things I didn't understand before. Somehow, my faith was stronger than ever. I began to talk aloud to Justin, to explain things to him, things I'd never had time to tell him. Though I couldn't see him anymore, I knew he was there.

"I admire you, my son, for having the courage to change your name. You recognized long before I did that my dad was not a good role model.

"I worried that my dad's cursing wishes had caused you to be taken from me so early. But I realize now that God doesn't work like that. Rain falls on the good and the evil, and just wishing doesn't make things so. Now, I have my courage.

"I'm sorry I cheated you, my own son, out of all the time I wasted! Now, I look back and see what a better parent I could have been for you. How much more time we could have spent together! How many wonderful things I could have taught you, had I known them at that time!

"And I know my sins were not taken out on you. That's not how God works, either. I'll remember all the good things, all the blue tulip memories. I remember the last time I saw you at the airport, waving good-bye with a couple of bucks in your hand and a tear in your eye. But you're gone. I'll have to live without you, at least for a while."

Once Charlie and I left California, we remained in a state of disbelief. We just stayed at home. We couldn't go anywhere, not even to church. There was too much crying and sadness within us. So, we sat home, my husband and I, not talking much, just staring. Sometimes, we'd put on the TV, leaving on *Wheel of Fortune*, news, or *Animal Planet* so as to have something in the background, something that didn't make us think.

Sleep was blackness. Go to bed, wake up. I used to dream before, but it was all just blackness now. The grief was too deep, too profound.

Then, one morning at about four, I awoke with tears all over my face and pillow. I was kind of laughing and smiling. I wanted to go back to sleep and finish my great dream. I tried to fall back asleep.

But something told me that it was more than a dream. Something told me to get out of bed and write it down before I forgot. *Oh, let me sleep and redream this! Let me stay here in this dream.* I tried so hard to sleep again, but I knew I had to get up and write this down. So I did. I pulled myself out of bed, crying all the time with joy as I wrote down the beautiful dream that I knew wasn't just a dream. The following is what I wrote.

It was Christmas Eve, but Charlie and I had no tree up, no lights, no decorations but for the Nativity scene outside, just something to honor the Lord.

We were all too sad to do much else. Nothing seemed to have any meaning that year. All of us were depressed and filled with such profound grief.

We sat in the front room, all of us, Sarah, me, Charlie, Young Charlie, Jules, and the twins, Olivia and Helena. We were all talking about past times with our Justin. Tears were flowing, and gloom filled the room. Jules just kept saying, "I'm so mad." I sat in one chair, and Sarah sat in another, across the room from me. Charlie and young Charlie were on the couch, and Jules sat in the red chair in the corner. The twins fell asleep on the floor. We were just exhausted from crying.

Then I heard the ADT alarm ring. Before it sounded a warning, someone punched in the code numbers, shutting the alarm off.

"Hey, you guys! What's going on?" It was Justin. It was Justin! He was dressed in light pants and a light red plaid shirt with rolled-up sleeves. I'd never seen him in those clothes before, and I thought he should have a coat on because it was really cold outside.

He asked, "Hey, where are the tree and the lights? It's Christmas, time to celebrate!"

I said, "It's not Christmas without you."

He said, "You're not without me. I'm here."

"I know, but you're gone, you're gone."

He came over to hug me, and I told him I missed him.

"I'm not gone, Mom. I know you miss me. It's alright. I love you, Mom."

Jules stood up, ready to fight. "I'm so mad! I'm so mad at you!"

He went over to Jules and said, "What're you so mad about?" He put his hands around her head and kissed her forehead.

She looked him in the eyes, and a big smile came over both of their faces. She said, "Nothing. Oh, my brother, I love you!"

He said, "I know, Jules, I know. I love you, too."

Young Charlie got teary-eyed and said, "Hey, I went roller skating for you last week. I thought about you the whole time and wore the shirt you gave me last year. I skated just for you."

"I know; I was there. You were great Young Charlie I saw it all."

Charlie got up and hugged Justin. Charlie was crying and couldn't say anything. Justin hugged him and said, "Love you, my man," to his dad.

Justin sat beside Sarah. I don't know how. The brown chair holds only one person.

I heard him say, "Baby, I love you." She cried, and he told her not to cry. He said, "Hey, we're having a baby. I'm so happy."

"But there's no money and how, how—"

He shushed her questions. She put her head next to his, and he ran his fingers through her hair, telling her how beautiful she was. "You're giving me the baby we wanted."

He kept telling her not to worry, that she wasn't alone and would never be alone. He spent most of the time with her. I didn't hear much of what he said to her. But I did hear him say, "I could never have been this happy without you … and our own child."

I noticed that there was a tree filled with lights, very bright lights. The only light in the room was from the tree. Small presents were under it. The light woke the twins, who had been sleeping on the floor.

"Uncle Justin! Daddy said you went to heaven." They both sat with him, and Sarah and I heard them ask if he had angel wings and if they could they see him fly. He laughed. Sarah laughed, too, as she kissed him. He told them that it wasn't exactly like that in heaven. They asked if they could go with him to see, and he said not right then, but later. He'd come back to show them.

Then, he said it was time to go.

Sarah got up and hugged Justin. She wasn't crying anymore. Jules was smiling as Justin hugged her. Young Charlie hugged him and said, "Ruffff," with tears in his eyes.

Charlie came over and said, "Son, I love you."

Justin reached into his pocket and pulled out two silver dollars. "Here's a couple of bucks, my man."

Charlie smiled. He couldn't say anything, because he was crying so much.

Justin came to me and again said, "Mom, I love you."

I hugged him. I don't remember him leaving, but he was no longer in the room with us.

I sat down and closed my eyes, but the light from the tree was too bright for me to sleep. I could smell the pine tree and cinnamon candles and a turkey cooking. I knew I'd have to get up and check on the turkey, but I think I fell asleep in the chair for a few minutes.

Then suddenly, I was awake and Justin was gone. The tree was gone. The scent of Christmas pine and cooking turkey was still in the air. But I didn't have a turkey in the oven. I had nothing at all cooking. I had no candles or pines, either.

I looked around. Everyone was sleeping. Sarah had her head tilted to the side as if someone was holding her, and her arms were formed in an embrace. She was smiling, almost laughing, and I saw a few tears fall down her cheeks.

Jules had curled in a ball on the chair. She had a big smile on her face, too.

Young Charlie was on the floor holding Olivia and Helena. They were all sleeping. Helena rolled over and laughed before falling back to sleep.

I thought I saw angel wings on the twins.

Charlie opened his eyes just about the same time as I did. We looked at each other and were smiling so hard that we were almost laughing. Then we actually were laughing hard. Happy tears fell freely.

Charlie reached into his pocket and pulled out two silver dollars. He looked at me and shook his head in disbelief. I agreed.

We were speechless.

And that was the dream. Of course, I wanted to go back to sleep to relive the whole thing, just to stay suspended in that dream. But I was too excited, too happy.

I knew then that it was okay. My boy was okay. Jesus had let him out of heaven for a little while to ease our pain and let us know that he was in good hands. It helped. I knew everything would be alright.

My son Charlie called me very early one morning and told me that he'd had a dream. He said he dreamed he saw Justin all shining with an amber light around him. In his dream, Charlie approached Justin. Justin said, "It's alright, Charlie. I'm okay. I'm okay."

Charlie called in the morning another time and told me that he had dreamed of being frightened in the night. Then, he said he dreamed that he climbed into bed with Justin, just like he used to do as a kid. Justin had assured him that everything would be alright, that he was safe with Justin.

Sarah had a dream that she saw Justin glowing before flying up to heaven like a shooting star.

She also said that she heard his voice one day as she was sleeping. He said, "It's okay."

She found herself answering, "But it's not okay. You're not here."

Many times after that, when I've have a difficult or sad day, I've awakened the next morning to find a different song in my head, one that answers the questions that bothered me the day before. For instance, I'll hear "You'll Never Walk Alone," "I Believe," and "Looking through the Eyes of Love." I don't consciously think of any songs or find myself listening to music these days. It isn't usual for me to awake with songs in my head. So, I take all these as signs, signs that Justin is safe with Jesus in heaven.

I dreamed that I saw him sitting on his painting scaffold, an old one that his paternal grandfather made a long time ago. He was all dressed in his white paint clothes, sitting on a cloud and looking down. Smiling in a knowing way and so brightly, looking down at us, Justin was so happy.

"We'll all be together again, Mom. You'll see."

I awoke one day with a kind of song that I'd never heard before. 'How bright I am, how much I see, how much I am.'

I told everyone about my dreams that were more than dreams. I take comfort in knowing that they were signs. I try to get closer in my relationship to Jesus so He will let me into heaven, too, when it's my time.

If you love to be near the water, if you love swimming, scuba diving, fishing, or sailing, then you move near the water. You go there every chance you get. That's what I'm doing, moving near the water, the cool clear water, the living water.

And now I have the answers to all—well most—of my questions. God does want Sarah to have the baby. God doesn't want to hurt us. He loves us. He wants us to love each other. "In that way you will be acting as true children of your Father in heaven. For He gives His sunlight to both the evil and the good, and He sends rain on the just and the unjust too" (Matthew 5:45).

"For God so loved the world he gave his only son" (John 3:16).

That's a lot more love than I could give.

Given that we human beings all treat God our Father poorly, if I were God, then I'd choose not to let my son be crucified for us. I'd just let all people blow themselves up. But that would mean me and my whole family, too! And I don't want that to happen.

So, I am glad I'm not God.

What a wonderful God we have, and how grateful I am that He gave me Justin, if only for those few years. I know He loves my son even more than I do, and I can hardly comprehend that. But I know He is taking care of my boy.

And for all the sorrow and pain that Justin's neighbor caused, I leave her to God. The money she took from my son will bring about her own demise. And she'll pay dearly for the grief she caused Justin and so many other innocent people. My own vengeance couldn't even come close to what God has planned.

Eternity is a long, long time.

And my dad, I leave him to God, also. I still pray for his soul. I hope he can change before it's too late.

I'm satisfied with all that God has given me. I still praise Him. I know that my whole family will spend a joyful eternity together. I thank God for my brothers and sisters, who have been invaluable all these years. I'm sorry I hadn't seen that before.

My friend Shirlene Baker sent me this prayer that helped me a lot:

God has not abandoned you.

He was patiently waiting for you to find this out all on your own. He wants you to give your love freely, not because you have to.

As we begin to seek God every day through His work and through prayer, He begins to give us a new perspective of contentment in this life. His greatest desire is that we love Him and seek Him above all else, and that we love others as He has loved us. God and people's souls are the only things that are going to last for eternity.

For the unseen things like faith, hope, and love are the things that are eternal and the only things that have true value in this life

When we begin to believe and speak the Word, it begins to transform us. The lives we live will begin to challenge the norm.

You may feel that you are just not measuring up to others' expectations or that you just don't have what it takes to be a person of whom your Creator as His masterpiece. And He has great plans and purposes for your life, even today.

Thanks, Shirlene, for that and also for all your words of wisdom. I think it's important to find the right role models. I wish I'd known Shirlene in the old days.

I look back and can see that there were some people in my life who would have been good role models, but I didn't recognize them as such at the time. So, I'm writing now to let others know not to let anyone hold you back. If something doesn't feel right, then it probably isn't. Find out. Open your mouth! Ask questions. If you get no answers that make sense, then keep looking.

Keep peace with your brothers and sisters. Don't let yourself be abused by anyone.

This is my story. This is the truth. I hope you can gain some insight into your own life and that this book helps you in some way.

Summary

*I*n the beginning, when Justin left this world, I wondered how God could know how I felt. I thought He couldn't know what it was like to lose a beloved son.

But I stopped when I heard Him say, "I do know. I did lose my Son. I gave Him up for you and your son."

Was Jesus really God?

Oh yes. I know that.

As a mother, I can understand that Mary knew that Jesus was God. Most any mother in her situation would have jumped in and tried to stop those people from killing Jesus. She could have thrown rocks or tried to start a riot, tried to kill them all or would have died trying. Many a mother would give her life for her child. I would have let them take my own life rather than let my child be hurt.

But this wasn't just any child. This was the Son of God. And Mary knew it. She knew it. She knew that He had to be crucified. She would do nothing to change God's will. And so she let it be.

Before realizing this, I never could understand why the apostles were so sad and depressed after Jesus was crucified. I couldn't understand that their faith was tested. I kept thinking that they should have known better, knowing that Jesus opened the gates of heaven for us. They knew His promises. But when grief comes upon you, it shakes your faith to some degree, no matter who you are. But you just have to hold on.

And His promises are true. My son is in heaven with Him. I know because Jesus said that whatever you pray for would be granted if it was

His Father's will. And it is God's will that all of us be with Him forever in heaven.

I tried to change on my own without inviting God into my life. Nothing I did worked. All the philosophy, whiskey, witchcraft, and toughness were dead-end solutions. I'm convinced that there's only one way people can change, and that is by allowing God to live in their hearts. Let Him lead the way. Jesus is your best role model.

"You are a reflection of the object of your affection." I read it somewhere; I can't remember where. Too bad I hadn't read it when I was younger, but then, I'd have been too dumb or arrogant to understand it.

It's also really important to know that all moms and dads are not automatically good role models. I wasn't. I thought I was a good mother, but thinking that I was, was not enough. I really didn't know how to be a good role model. And certainly my parents weren't either. I was convinced that I and my sisters and brothers were as worthless as we'd been told we were. I believed that none of us would ever amount to anything.

I watched as my cousins became doctors, pilots, business owners. They took time and learned their skills. There were no short cuts. But me, I never allowed myself any dreams. I know, I know. It's time to stop that. Of course, it was my own fault. I should have known better then.

But I know better now. I no longer feel compelled to put myself on trial. I know that the only one who will judge me is God. And thank God that He is merciful!

I told you what you need to know. Now, you're on your own. Go on your search. You'll find Him if you are brave enough to see.

I'm not scared anymore. It took a long time, but I finally found out that it's not a good idea to listen to someone tell you, "Don't say anything! Don't start any trouble!" Say what you need to say before it's too late. If you're wrong, then find it out right away. Don't wait till it's all bottled up inside you and it's too late.

I'm all grown up. And free. Thank God that my eyes were opened before it was too late. I now understand.

"Though it makes Him sad to see the way we live, He'll always say, I forgive."

Epilogue, 2014

*I*t's been over a year now since my son left this world. My heart has learned to live in two worlds, one here on earth and another in heaven with my boy. I had a mural done of Justin, looking as I saw him look in heaven. It gives me comfort to see it every day. Prayer comes easy to me now, every day, every minute. I pray when I want to. I pray when I don't want to. I find myself praying while I'm watching television. Sometimes, tears overcome me like a rogue wave on the sea. I let myself drown in the sorrow. Then just as the rogue wave recedes, I bob up to the surface to find that I'm okay again. I take a deep breath and, while waiting for the next wave to come over me, thank God for letting me have Justin for those years he had on earth. I thank Him for my other kids, for my husband, for my family, for sunlight, for everything. I find I've become one of those fanatics, and it's okay with me.

One day, Sarah was looking for a parking space. She usually found one in that area, but this time there was nothing. She traveled a few more blocks farther and then spotted one. As she pulled in, she noticed something unusual, a little glint in the sun near her parking meter. She went over to see what it was and saw a tiny music box with a little gold angel on it. She turned the key and it played "Lara's Theme" ("Somewhere, my love"). She picked it up, held it close, and whispered, "Thank you, oh, thank you."

A gift from heaven …

Sarah has continued her plan to have the family that she and Justin wanted. Charlie and I pray constantly for those little embryos, part

Justin part Sarah. We pray for our future grandchildren. May Jesus grant them life.

My saintly aunt June died a few weeks ago. (It's strange that I can write that *d* word for someone else, and yet for my Justin, well, I still can only say that he's gone.) I went to visit my auntie when she was sick, before the end. I told her that I would gladly trade places with her. She joked and said that I was just jealous that she would see Justin before I did. "You're right," I said. We laughed. Hers was a feeble laugh. She knew the time was near. She was a good soul who was looking forward to going home to Jesus.

My dad, her brother, came to the funeral home. The first thing he did was point to my oldest sister, Helen and loudly say that he wished it were her in that casket. He talked about his money the whole time.

My dad turned ninety-four last week. Sadie, Helen, and Martha took him out for a luncheon with his old girlfriend, Millie. He said that his birthday wish was that he'd outlive all his kids. 'My wish is to see you all rolling on the ground sucking for air.' Then he continued to tell the people who were there that all his life his kids tried to steal his money because they were all jealous of him.

Dad calls Jack at least twice a week complaining and telling him that it was my mother's fault that he had all of us. "Women should know how to prevent stuff like that. I'll never forgive her for that. I could've been a happy man without all of you." In Dad's view, Jack and the rest of us will always be just "stuff like that."

I pray in Jesus's name that God may break the curse my father has put on the families of all of his children.

Thank you for reading my story. God bless you.